Essential Skills for
The Occasional Genealogist

Beyond-beginner Genealogy Skills
for Busy Family Historians

by Jennifer Patterson Dondero

Wait!

Before you start reading,

download the free digital bonuses.

If you're anything like me, you've slapped a genealogy how-to book onto a photocopier to get a copy of a worksheet or template only to get a poor copy.

Well, you don't have to with this book.

Sign-up once and I'll email you the links to access all the bonus material for the book:

https://genealogyskills.com/bonus/

ISBN: 979-8-88759-945-8 - paperback

ISBN: 979-8-88759-946-5 - ebook

This book is dedicated to my family. They've put up with a lot when "I have to write."

TABLE OF CONTENTS

Introduction

Hi, I'm Jennifer, and I'm an Occasional Genealogist. I never have enough time to do genealogy; I only *occasionally* get to do it. Or rather, I only occasionally get to do my own research. I have been a professional genealogist since 2005, but since starting to work for myself in 2008, I've spent most of my genealogy time on clients' research, not my own.

Are You an Occasional Genealogist?

Most hobbyist genealogists I talk to consider themselves Occasional Genealogists. Most professional genealogists I talk to are also Occasional Genealogists! So many things vie for our time, it's hard to find enough time for our own genealogy research, regardless if genealogy is only your hobby or your profession.

Hobbyist Versus Professional

The main difference between being a hobbyist and a professional isn't your research knowledge. Many hobbyists have professional-level knowledge. The difference is knowing where to spend your time. Spending more time now—on the right things—gets you to a solution sooner.

Professionals quickly learn this. They ethically need to spend time on certain things hobbyists sometimes consider a waste of time. Even when new professionals don't understand why this ethical necessity exists, they learn from experience. As a hobbyist genealogist, you can skip spending time on anything you want. If you consistently skip certain actions, you will never learn their value from experience. Being educated on the value of these steps may convince you it's worth spending your limited genealogy time on what you might have seen as "just for professionals."

Great Genealogy for All

This book covers the essential skills you need for great genealogy. That's great genealogy whether you are researching for your own pleasure or want to be a professional. Great genealogy is how you succeed in your research.

Genealogical success is the same for hobbyists or professionals. Both want to solve a genealogical problem. Both want to find the correct ancestors and the correct information about them.

If you aren't interested in success, if your standard is simply a huge tree regardless of its accuracy, you don't need to do great genealogy. You don't need to do genealogy at all. You can simply make-up names, dates, and places.

So, throughout this book, I'm assuming you are interested in finding the correct ancestors and the correct information for them. It doesn't matter if you're seeking your ancestors, your spouse's, your in-law's, a friend's, a client's, or anyone else's ancestors. Whatever starting person you have, you want to find their ancestors and identify the correct relationships and information.

This may seem like a silly point to make. Would anyone start reading a genealogy book if they weren't interested in finding the correct names, dates, and places? Probably not. But it's an important concept to keep in mind when you start questioning if all the work of genealogy is necessary. If you're wondering if you need to do something described in this book, you can ask yourself if you're interested in the correct names, dates, places, and relationships or if you're interested in merging any two people of the same or similar name so you have names, dates, and places in your tree without making them up.

The Consequences of Not-great Genealogy

I've never met a genealogist that wants the wrong person in their tree. I've met many who research as if they do. Great genealogy minimizes errors which means you are building the correct family tree. We all make mistakes. When you take the time for great genealogy, you are able to correct your mistakes before you build branch onto branch of your family tree. Building branches onto the wrong person means those branches aren't for the ancestors of your root person.

The consequences of sloppy genealogy are making one error in identifying a person in your family tree and then successfully finding their ancestors. The ancestors of the incorrect person are not your ancestors. One wrong person branches into more and more errors.

Of course, this doesn't always happen. Sometimes, instead, you mix information about your ancestor and other people of the same or similar names. In this case, you don't keep building the wrong person's tree. In this situation, you're stuck because you're trying to research a non-existent person.

Rushing genealogy leads to building the wrong tree or being perpetually stuck. The consequences of not-great genealogy are pretty severe.

Modern Genealogy

Rushing genealogy was less of an issue in the past. Not because researchers were so much more careful. In the past, all genealogy work was much slower. You could not pop a name in an online search form and get results. You had to go places or write and receive information by mail. You had to read records, not digitally search them. This did make genealogists more careful, but it also allowed fewer people to do genealogy. It was a hobby for retirees or others without significant responsibilities on their time. The internet and online research have completely changed who can do genealogy. It changed how you access records—but not how you do genealogy.

Unfortunately, technology has changed faster than genealogy education. Problems in genealogy can take years to appear. It's a long-term hobby. It's not like knitting a scarf where you can pause and see you dropped a stitch. The equivalent small error in genealogy, one that could unravel your work, might not become apparent for days, weeks, months, or years.

Great teachers didn't want to teach flawed methods as 21st-century technology became available. To avoid this, or because they were still learning the technology themselves, the same process was taught in 2010 as in 1960. You'd type in documents instead of writing on paper, though. Teaching great genealogy teaches a slow process. Today's genealogists didn't get started because they had so much time on their hands, as was more likely in the past. Most are busy; they are Occasional Genealogists. Modern genealogists wanted modern shortcuts to fit their time.

Problems With Modern Shortcuts

Some parts of genealogy are done the way they always have been. You're just using a digital method instead of paper. But other tasks can be sped up using a different digital method, methods that don't have a paper equivalent. Using technology is not a problem in itself. The problem is digital methods that seem to be a shortcut but are actually a dropped stitch. They will unravel your work in the future.

The Plight of the Occasional Genealogist

This is the plight of the Occasional Genealogist. You don't have enough time for your research. You don't want to use 20th-century techniques. But some modern shortcuts cause problems. How do you speed up the process without incorporating issues that will unravel your work?

I've had the unusual situation of being a professional genealogist, an Occasional Genealogist, and for a short time, an often genealogist. I've learned Occasional Genealogy needs to be explained differently. That's why I started my blog, *The Occasional Genealogist*, not to write about my experiences but to help *all* the Occasional Genealogists out there learn how to do great genealogy, despite the interruptions. I want you to know which shortcuts to use and which to avoid.

By the way, I'm *an* Occasional Genealogist, not *the* Occasional Genealogist. The blog is *for* the Occasional Genealogist, which means for you! If I had wanted the blog to be about me, I would have called it *An Occasional Genealogist* because I know I'm not the only one.

Learn to Do Great Genealogy

In this book, I want to help you learn to do great genealogy, despite the interruptions. A book allows me to ensure you get the full foundation you need. That's not something I can do via the blog, where the format is short pieces of content you pick and choose from.

What This Book Is and Is Not

A book is a terrible way to give you step-by-step instructions when images would help, especially if technology is involved. A book is much harder to keep updated than online content, after all. So this book is foundational, but it won't go in-depth on topics better explained with online videos or images, as you'd find in one of *The Occasional Genealogist Academy* courses. What you'll learn from this book are tried-and-true techniques and strategies updated for 21st-century genealogists.

This book is not a step-by-step guide to doing technology tasks. I've provided links to some additional free resources every 21st-century genealogist can use, but the focus is not on using technology. Technology is important to Occasional Genealogists, but we've been in the 21st-century long enough to have some tried-and-true options that don't rely on shortcuts that are short-lived. Most of the technology-related information in this book can be applied with various apps or software. Pick technology you are comfortable with instead of learning the flavor of the month app.

This book also is not a list of problem-solving tips to pick and choose from—often called brick wall busters. You can find free lists of brick wall busters online. Many books on brick wall busters exist, too. Check your local library because these are pretty popular. In fact, you don't need a 21st-century guide if what you want are brick wall busters. How you access genealogy records has changed, but the problem-solving tips are the same as they were in the 20th-century.

This book is for the time-strapped genealogist that wants to know how to do great genealogy. You aren't satisfied with being handed a fish—a solution to one genealogy problem.

You want to know how to fish and probably make your own rod and net to boot.

Let Me Tell You a Story

I've been trying to write this book, about doing great genealogy, despite the interruptions, for quite a while. But here's the thing, it's not the most exciting topic to explain and, therefore, to read. Once you have all the parts, how it changes your research is very exciting. But if you only get half the story, it's a lot less exciting.

So that's what I will give you, a whole story. We often use case studies in genealogy, but those aren't stories. They are a variation on a brick wall buster but more in-depth. This book isn't a case study. It does have a genealogy story to tell.

I'm going to tell you a story about Imogene ("Gene") and her friend Virginia ("Jenni," a more common spelling of Gini). Jenni's genealogy research has gotten quite stuck. Gene's going to help her out. A case study in genealogy doesn't show you what didn't work, but you'll get to see what Jenni has tried and how Gene suggests she try something else. Although Imogene and Virginia are fictional, the examples come from real-life. No one has all these problems (I hope), but it is helpful to see what isn't working instead of only being told what you should do. Because I'm going to show failure, not just success, it was a good idea to fictionalize the genealogists involved!

Using This Book

The book is broken into three sections. Section one is your starting place. You may wish to stop after reading it and practice what you've learned. The book is broken up this way purposely because many genealogy concepts become clearer once you practice them.

Section two goes deeper. Some genealogists may find this content more than they are ready for. If this is you, I'd suggest reading it and then perhaps going back over section one and continuing to practice the concepts in section one. You can't learn to do great genealogy by reading only one book. You can't learn to do great genealogy by taking only one course, even if that course spanned a year.

More advanced concepts take time to sink in, and some won't stick until you get actual experience with them. Just because the material doesn't click the first time you learn it doesn't mean you can't learn it. You can do this! Give yourself permission to gain experience and improve over time.

The third section is a little different. I felt additional topics were needed so you could practice what was covered in sections one and two. These didn't seamlessly fit into the progression covered in the first two sections. I've written section three as if you've read sections one and two. You can try reading section three's chapters out of order, though. Sections one and two build on each other. They need to be read in order, don't skip around.

Also, make sure you grab the downloadable bonus material. Not everything fits neatly in a book. The bonus material includes a digital template you can use.

If you didn't sign-up already, get the bonus material at: https://genealogyskills.com/bonus/

Why Gene and Jenni?

By the way, since we're all genealogists here, I thought you'd like to know that Imogene and Virginia are two of my kids' great-grandmothers, one from each side of the family. I was trying to think of genealogy-themed names for my two characters, but I had only heard one, "Jenny Genie." Suddenly I realized those great-grandmothers went by Jean and Jenny when they were girls. It seemed a good way to honor my grandmother and my husband's grandmother by naming my fictional genealogists, Gene and Jenni.

If you get the two characters mixed up, because their names are similar, remember, Gene is the more experienced *Gene*alogist.

Gene and Jenni's Story and Research— Don't Miss It!

You'll find Jenni and Gene's story at the beginning of each chapter. *Don't skip the story.* Gene shares lots of great tips! After the story, get more in-depth instruction from me. Many of the chapters include examples from Jenni's research. These examples are intentionally hobbyist examples, not examples from my professional research. I have included some examples from my research, but I've tried not to format them using professional standards unless it was an extra variation for you to see.

When I was only a hobbyist, I often found professional examples distracted me. Sometimes I'd get focused on trying to perfect a format that was just for professionals. Other times I tried to drop something important because I erroneously thought it was just for professionals. I've seen the same thing when interacting with my blog readers. I didn't recognize much of what was important from professional examples until I had mastered the concept. I've tried to improve your foresight by giving you realistic examples instead of perfect examples.

Are you ready to get started with Gene and Jenni's story?

Section 1: Essentials to Get You Started

Chapter 1:
What's Your Problem?

Imogene was navigating her cart through Publix, trying to figure out which aisle had ramen noodles. Were they with the Asian foods or with pasta? Her grandkids were coming tomorrow, and that was one food she knew they would eat if she could find it.

As her cart left the international foods aisle, she had to stop suddenly.

"Ahhh!" she gasped, "Jenni! I almost hit you." Her friend Virginia had passed in front of her cart as if she hadn't seen her.

"Oh, Gene, I didn't see you there."

"Yes, that was obvious. Is something wrong? You look a little more lost than you should be in a grocery store."

"I'm sorry," Virginia said. "It's nothing. I need to get moving. I'm supposed to make spaghetti for James's boys' night tonight. I've been so distracted, I completely forgot, and there isn't a noodle in the house."

Gene looked at Jenni's empty cart, which had come from the direction of the pasta aisle. "Why don't you walk with me? I need some noodles, too. You can tell me what's so distracting you can't buy spaghetti without a crash."

Jenni turned her cart around so the two women could head in the right direction. "It's silly, really. You know I started my family history a few years ago after my mother died?"

"Yes, I remember."

"Well, I found some interesting information, but then I got busy and haven't had time to get back to it."

"OK." Gene was wondering how this led to a cart crash.

"For my birthday, James gave me a subscription to that online site, so I finally got going again. But now I'm stuck. I found some more information, but I can't seem to find any more ancestors. I've been wracking my brain trying to think what else I can do. It's driving me crazy!"

Gene laughed. "Yeah, I've had a few brick walls drive me nuts, too. Maybe I can help you. I had a cousin who had done a lot of research, and it helped to talk over problems with her, even if I was working on a different branch of the family than we shared. She told me having a genealogy buddy to discuss things was one of her secret weapons."

Gene and Jenni agreed to meet on Monday and went their separate pasta cooking ways.

Takeaway: It never hurts to have another set of eyes on a genealogy problem. Find a genealogy buddy or several. Your local genealogy society is a great place to find a local buddy. You can be virtual buddies with family or friends that live farther away.

***

Monday rolled around, and Gene was standing on Jenni's porch, knocking on her front door.

"Come in!" she heard through the open door. Gene opened the screen and went in. Jenni sat at a desk on one side of the room, leaning forward, peering intently at her monitor. Jenni's usually immaculately coiffed white and silver hair looked rather limp and abused. Gene suspected Jenni had repeatedly run her hands through it in frustration.

The large screen was full of search results from Jenni's gifted subscription site. Gene was quite familiar with the site. She was also familiar with the genealogist lost in her search.

"Sit down," Jenni invited, waving at an adjacent chair without taking her eyes off the results she was scanning. She ran her left hand through her hair, making it stick up strangely. Gene reached up automatically and ran her hand through her dark, short cut as if adjusting her own hair would fix Jenni's.

Gene could tell Jenni had a terrible case of genealogy-itis. Normally, Jenni was quite the hostess. Gene had never been to Jenni's house when snacks weren't at the ready, sometimes even a homemade cake. Gene, on the other hand, tended to be all business. Jumping straight to why she was there was fine with her, although if she was going to watch Jenni stare at the monitor, cake would make it more interesting. Oh, well.

Gene watched Jenni pore over the results. She kept scrolling and scrolling, clearly not finding anything that interested her. Finally, she sighed and sat back, shaking her hair almost back into place. She looked at Gene.

"Sorry. I guess I got a little wrapped up in this. I wanted to try to do it on my own one more time before you got here." Jenni looked a bit tired now that Gene could see her face. How long had she been staring at that screen? Her eyes looked dry. She had clearly put on lipstick at some point, but most of it seemed to be missing. Gene realized she'd never seen Jenni without her lipstick. This was serious.

"No problem, Jenni. So tell me about your problem. Is this the person you're stuck on?" Gene asked, indicating the monitor.

"Yes. Well, one of them. This is my great-grandfather Jones. I think my cousins found the wrong death for him." Jenni palmed the mouse and clicked another tab, "But here's another great-grandfather, Henry Alford. I can't find his father to save my life." Jenni clicked another tab, "This is my German line. I can find her parents but not his." Jenni clicked another tab, "And this one's just a mess!"

Jenni smiled at Gene as if to say, *it's pretty bad, right? You understand.* Gene sat, overwhelmed by all Jenni was trying to do. Finally, she spoke.

"Um, Jenni, how long have you had these tabs open? I mean, how long have you been working on this?" Gene gestured at the monitor. "Is this all from this morning?"

"Yes. James can be a stickler about shutting the computer down every night. It drives me nuts. I wish I could leave everything on the screen so I don't have to keep starting over. I can only get through about five pages of results per person—when I'm working on the whole family—before I have to do something else. If I don't return later in the day, James shuts down the computer at night, and I have to start over the next time."

Gene nodded, "Yes, I can see that would be frustrating. Do you always work on all these problems at once?"

"No. But I don't have much time to spend on the computer. I try to work on all of them a few times a week so I don't forget what I did before. I think I'll be able to do more this winter when it's too cold to be outside. That will help."

Gene wasn't sure where to start to help Jenni. She decided this was a good time to start at the beginning and not worry about what would come later.

"Jenni, I think you need to start focusing on one project at a time. Genealogy is hard. You can't work on two problems at the same time."

"Sure I can. I do it all the time."

"No, you switch between projects all the time. You can't literally work on two at the same time." Gene thought before she spoke, "Have you heard of context switching?" Jenni shook her head in the negative, so Gene went on. "Context switching is when you switch between tasks. We often think we're multi-tasking, but you can't literally do too many things simultaneously. People switch from one task to another or switch thinking about one thing and then another. That's OK if it's something easy, like doing the laundry and catching up on a TV show. Neither of those requires a lot of thought.

"It's pretty easy to keep up with the show if you don't have to think about how to wash the clothes. If you have to think about the settings for the laundry, you aren't paying as much attention to the show. Which is fine; it's just entertainment.

"But you're switching between different genealogy problems. It's all genealogy, but the problems are different, and they are all hard. You have to stop what you were thinking about and switch gears." Gene could tell from the look on Jenni's face she wasn't convinced.

Gene took a breath and continued, hoping this important concept would sink in with one more example. "It's like riding a bike. Every time you context switch, it's like starting up a hill. Switching from TV to laundry is a little hill. Switching from laundry to TV might be a slightly bigger hill. Switching from one hard genealogy project to another is a big hill. You're never letting yourself get to the top. You're starting over, going up the hill from a dead stop at the bottom each time you change projects, especially since you don't appear to have any notes to help you catch back up." Gene had noticed the spotlessly clean desk and that nothing else was open on the computer besides the tabs Jenni had shown her. That was one of the issues that would have to wait, though.

"Do you understand what I'm saying?"

"Yes, I think so. My brain is starting over—thinking about the problem anew each time I switch back and forth."

"That's it."

"But doesn't the computer do some of the work for me? It finds the records."

Gene loved answering this question. "Well, that's why you were able to do as much as you have. But the computer isn't that good at genealogy. It can do the easy stuff faster than you because it finds records matching your search. Once you need records that aren't as good a match, you, the human, need to decide what's best." Jenni looked mildly bewildered, so Gene went on, "Let's not worry about that. Just realize the computer helped when research was easy, but now the research has gotten harder. Humans are much better at harder genealogy problems than computers, and that's where you are. Let's look at the problems you want to focus on and decide which one I can help you with."

In the next section, you can learn about the W-frame System Gene taught Jenni for defining one problem you want to work on. Then you can see examples before you try the System for yourself.

***

Why Define Your Problem

Context switching is a real thing, not something Gene made up. Because of the amount of thought you need to put into a hard genealogy project, switching from one project to another will cause you to waste time because your brain thinks it is continually restarting a new problem. If you're short on time, you will get better results by focusing on one thing at a time.

Later, we'll look at the other skills to keep you moving forward on all your projects without working on *all* of them every time you try to research. For now, focus on focus. Define your problem with the W-frame System so you can focus on one problem at a time.

The W-frame System is easy to remember and makes sure you have all the details needed for the single problem you've chosen to work on. If you lack some of the details, trying to find them distracts you. Finding the details is a different problem; it's not the problem you intended to focus on. Even this seemingly minor issue requires your brain to switch from thinking about how to solve that problem to the specifics which define your problem, such as where to find the dates, places, and maybe even names. It's one problem, but your brain has to context switch between different activities related to the problem.

Without the details the W-frame System requires, you might struggle to progress, which is no fun. Using the W-frame System is a quick and easy way to ensure you are ready and can focus on your chosen project.

The W-frame System

The W-frame System is simply the four classic "W" questions you learned in school for writing papers or for journalism, plus a reminder W. The Ws have been tweaked to focus on one brick wall problem—a difficult genealogy problem. Here are the brick wall W questions:

Who is the subject of my problem—one person, couple, or family as is appropriate for your what?

What one event or relationship is my problem about?

When does the event or relationship take place—your time frame?

Where does the event occur, or where does the person live during the *when*—this can be one or more places.

Plus... **Write** it down—as in, the answers to these four questions need to be written down.

That's it, *who, what, when,* and *where,* then write. You must answer all four of these questions before working on a problem. If you can't answer one of them, you are not ready to work on that problem. Instead, you need to work on a problem that will provide the missing W element.

When you're missing one of the four W elements, often you need to back up your research to focus on the previous research leading to asking this question. This is one of the reasons the W-frame System works so well. It helps you focus, but it also helps you realize you're trying to work on a problem prematurely. Once we discuss what that W-frame System does for you, the researcher, I've included some examples.

Note: You should always define your *who* by including their name, birth, and death information. It is standard in genealogy to include the birth and death information in parenthesis after their name if it is not being included otherwise. This information does not need to be complete dates and places. It is whatever estimate or partial information you have. You will see examples of this throughout the book.

The person's lifespan, their birth and death information, distinguishes the person of that name from another person of the same name. The purpose of always including the birth and death information is to know who is the subject of the problem clearly.

Imagine you handed the problem definition and all your existing research to someone (I mean *all* your research). Now imagine six people in your research, all with the same name, in different branches of your tree. How would this person find the research related to the correct *who*?

This is a good test to make sure you have defined your *who*, not just included a name. The point isn't to have every detail in your W-frame-defined problem, but you do need enough details to distinguish the subject of the project from someone else with the same name and possibly *similar* details. That's what genealogy research is, after all. Finding the right person in a sea of records.

When a W *Is* Your Problem

Are you wondering how the W-frame System can work if what you're looking for is a place or date? Don't worry! The W-frame System is so effective because it ensures you've got all the details for problems of any type. Before we learn more about the W-frame System, it's time to dive into what sounds like an intimidating genealogy topic.

Genealogical Analysis

Genealogical analysis can sound hard, boring, or academic, but it is something simple. You've already done it if you've successfully built your family tree. It's also crucial to on-going genealogical success. You cannot build *your* family tree without analysis. You can fill a tree with random names and dates, but we've already established this book is for people who want to build an accurate tree. That means you will need to do genealogical analysis.

If you've done more than attach someone else's tree to yours and called it done, you've performed analysis. Analysis, or analyzing, is breaking something down into its component parts. Different types of analyses exist in the world, and they are done differently. We will start with the most basic genealogical analysis—which you've already been doing.

The easiest way to break something down for family history is to ask questions. You can see this relates to the W-frame System since it's a series of questions. But you analyze by asking questions to begin your family history, "Who are my ancestors," or "Where did my family come from?" That was identifying what you wanted to do, but you couldn't do anything without breaking that question down. It required you to analyze the problem.

You can't answer, "where did my family come from?" out of thin air. It's not like asking, "What do I want for dinner?"

In that case, you search your brain for an answer. For family history, you probably asked something like one of these questions:

- What family member can I ask about where we came from?
- Which part of the family am I actually interested in?
- What was that site I saw on a TV commercial that said I could find my family tree?
- Did someone tell me there was a written family history?
- Wasn't there something hanging on Aunt Jun's wall that had something to do with Great-grandma's native village?
- What was that story Granny told us when we visited her in 1975? It was about where her family came from.

These are ways to break the main problem down. They are the absolute most basic genealogical analysis. The W-frame System is a list of questions, too, and a list of questions designed to further break your chosen problem into its components. It's a more effective type of analysis than random questions you come up with. It's still very basic genealogical analysis.

First Genealogy Analysis

Too many genealogists do the obvious type of breakdown, going from "where did my family come from" to "where did my great-grandfather Miller come from," but nothing more. You can stick some details about your great-grandfather into an online search form with that question. You can take action once you get to that question, so you keep taking that action. The more times you repeat the action, the fewer and fewer new and relevant results you get. If you want to get new or different results, you must learn to do further analysis so you can define a new problem.

So far, in our example, we went from asking, "where did my family come from" to "where did my great-grandfather Miller come from?" In this initial analysis, you have the *who* and *what* broken down. *Who* is great-grandfather Miller, you know his actual name to work on the problem, but it isn't important in this example. The *what* is where he came from. You are asking about his immigration or migration, which is the event you want to research.

If you have successfully researched this man, you likely also have basic *when* and *where*, just as you should have his whole name, not just his relationship to you and his surname. You probably used his estimated birthday as your *when* and either his birthplace or a place you know he lived as the *where* when you searched for him online.

The computer matched what you entered to records from the site you searched. Presumably, you have now reached a point where you need more records or results, but what you know is not providing more relevant search results.

It's uncommon to further analyze a person's name (the *who*). Sometimes you can, but normally genealogists learn about other name variations or nicknames in new records, or they learn about common nicknames. In other words, we don't obtain name information by analyzing what we already have; we either learn other options through education or find them with research.

However, maybe you've never thought about *who* you are researching. Perhaps if you think about great-grand-father Edward Miller, you realize he could be Ed or Ned or even Teddy Miller. In most cases, if you know that, you've already tried those alternatives. You already know how to do genealogical analysis and have been doing it if you've tried nicknames for a person.

You also often cannot analyze the *what* further. This can be a part of genealogical analysis, but it is more advanced. If you want to know where Grandpa Miller came from, that's what you want to know. You can try researching related problems, but coming up with alternatives is a more advanced option you get to after you learn to do basic genealogical analysis, such as with the W-frame System.

An essential analysis skill you need to start with is getting great at breaking down the *when* and *where*. Even when you want to find a date or place of an event, you can still answer all the W-frame questions. You *need* to answer all four W questions.

When that online search form stops giving you the answers you seek, you have to take the reins and analyze your problem. This means improving the *when* and *where* for your problem.

Analyzing When and Where

Every genealogical problem has a time frame and place, a *when* and *where*. I have yet to meet a genealogist who isn't working on a problem that involves the place of Earth. In fact, every genealogist I've worked with can identify a country or countries involved in their problem. That's a much more specific *where* than Earth.

If you're looking for a date or place, you want to start as close chronologically to that date or geographically close to the place as possible so you solve your problem faster. If you were looking for a place and started with Earth, you'd be considering research on any continent. If you can start with a country instead, you're considering far less research. If you can break your existing problem down to a more specific location, you've further limited the amount of research you need to do. Really, if you can't be more specific than a place of Earth, you aren't ready to research that problem!

Once you start every problem with the W-frame System, it's obvious how to estimate *when* and *where* for any project. But many 21st-century genealogists have a mindset like Jenni, believing the computer will search for them. Using the W-frame System reminds you to focus on the four main elements and break them down as much as possible before you start. It's a quick and easy way to fast-track your project and force you to focus.

When you ask yourself where your event takes place, if your problem involves one town, that's the place. Yes, you might learn other places are involved, but *start* with that one place. In contrast, you might have several places that are countries because you don't know precisely when and where the event took place. What you do know about the person involved still provides the place or places.

Most problems have *some* narrow locations, such as a region, county, parish, town, and so on,   even if another location is an entire country. You might know your ancestor lived in a certain town in the U.S. or part of a certain state and that they were born in a different country. That's more specific than using the whole U.S. and all of that other country.

For example, you might not know where a marriage took place. That's the event, the *what*, you want to find. With immigrant ancestors, you might not initially know if they married before or after arriving in the new country. You need to have at least one place for the couple, or one of them, near the time you think the marriage took place. If you don't, you aren't ready to work on that problem.

Here's an example of a problem where you need to start by backing up and doing additional research before focusing on your initial goal. You're looking for a place of marriage, and all you know is the husband was born in Germany, and both husband and wife died in California when they were in their 90s. That is a timeframe of over ninety years and quite a large geographical area, potentially the entire U.S. and Germany. You do not have a place near the time the marriage likely took place unless, of course, this is a marriage you know took place when the couple was over 80. If the marriage occurred that late in life, you have a date within twenty years of their last known residence.

Usually, we seek a marriage for our ancestral couple at an age that would allow her to have children, not in her 80s or 90s. The husband can be estimated to be at least 20 when he married, so we do *not* have a place within twenty years of the marriage using the information we have. The location of

Germany is at least twenty years before our earliest marriage estimate. The location of California is likely several decades from the marriage, as well. The locations we know are not good estimates for our *what*. Back up and perform simple research before trying to solve this problem.

The biggest 21st-century problem genealogists might face is thinking they can research any problem, no matter how much or little research they've previously done. In this marriage example, you may think you can just search genealogy websites because you have the names of the husband and wife. You have enough information to fill in an online search form. You might get lucky and find the marriage. Are you sure the record is for *your* couple and not a couple with the same names? How can you be sure if you only have names to go on? People are more than just names.

Let's look at how you could analyze a similar problem with a few more details.

Basic Analysis Example

Let's say you're looking for the marriage of John and Mary Obspts. You don't know Mary's maiden name; that's part of why you want to find the marriage! You do have some details on John and Mary from basic research. Let's say John was born in New York in about 1836, and Mary was born in North Carolina in about 1840. You know they both died in California, John in 1912, and Mary was still alive at that time. You descend from one of their sons, who was born in Illinois in about 1875. This is a lot more information than the previous example! You pop their names into a search form and can't find the marriage. You repeat this on every site you know with no luck. What now?

This is where you further analyze the problem. You have more details than in the previous example, so your next step is not backing up and doing further research. Your mind likely started analyzing this problem automatically.

Where do you think John and Mary married? New York, North Carolina, Illinois, California? They likely married in the U.S.! You have two options at this point, keep researching John and Mary, hoping a record gives details of their marriage. Or, you can analyze what you do know.

The child you descend from, the one you have information about, was born when Mary was around 35. He could be their first child, but it's more likely he is not. When you are analyzing the problem, you will make some assumptions. We'll talk more about this in section two. Part of analysis is making or considering assumptions.

You are assuming John and Mary married before your ancestor was born. You are assuming this is their first marriage. You are assuming they married as young adults, well before Mary was 35. These are not facts; we don't record our assumptions as facts like we'd record a date or place we found in a source. You need to make assumptions to do analysis. You continue to analyze changing these assumptions as you gain more information from research. It's essential to find the middle ground with these assumptions. Don't use assumptions instead of research. Don't avoid making assumptions at all.

A good assumption is something statistically likely based on what you know. You don't know or suspect your ancestor is illegitimate, so you assume he is legitimate. You don't know or suspect John or Mary had a previous marriage, so you assume this is their first marriage. In this time and place, a woman usually married in her late teens or early 20s. That means that age range is statistically likely for Mary.

Combining reasonable assumptions with information from research indicates John and Mary probably married well before your ancestor was born. That means you have no information about this couple around the time they likely married. You analyzed the problem. Unfortunately, you don't have enough information for a good W-frame-defined problem.

If your ancestor was born when Mary was about 20, his birthplace would have been an excellent *where* for your W-frame problem. But for our example, where Mary was about 35, you want more information from research. Instead of researching the marriage, you can take a step back and decide to work on a problem that will build your knowledge of this family.

The easy place to start in a problem like this is to see if other children appear in the census households. That is a very simple "step back" project which will refine your *possible* marriage place from the U.S. to something more specific. You should have already excluded California as a likely marriage place; that is a location after your ancestor was born. You can exclude New York, too. It was John's birthplace, and he was born before Mary. You are still considering locations between North Carolina and Illinois. You don't have information to allow you to be any more specific. Remember, you've already tried searching online without more specific information.

Once you look at census records, or look again, you might find six older children in the family. The oldest was born in Alabama or Mississippi, the next two in Louisiana, and finally, the next two in Mississippi or Kentucky. Just this information, without considering anything else, supports that you shouldn't be looking in New York, and you probably shouldn't look in North Carolina, and probably not in Illinois.

You can use information from U.S. census records to adjust the *when*. For this example, your records indicate—rather than "prove"—John and Mary married before the oldest child was born. You could try looking for searchable online marriage databases for Alabama and Mississippi as your next step, or you could continue working on the step back project to gather more information.

I would continue with the step back research in this case, but this is something I can decide based on my experience. Every genealogist has to work with their own experience level. Doing research gives you more experience, so sometimes you just have to do what you know you can do.

Mississippi can be a difficult state to research online. If the marriage did occur in Mississippi, the record might have been destroyed, it might never have been recorded, or it may need to be found offline. Researching in Mississippi can be more work. I'd rather do any remaining simple research on the family before I decide if I need to put extra effort into researching in Mississippi. I would make this decision based on my personal experience researching Mississippi records online. Someone with different experience, or different access to Mississippi records, might make an alternative decision.

Situations like this example happen all the time. Doing the most basic analysis to answer all four W questions will highlight when you are missing important details that *should* affect your next step. If this example had been different, where every child was born in Illinois, you might not continue the step back project until you searched for a marriage specifically in Illinois. If the example had been for a couple that was born and died in the same place, you could have used that location as a starting estimate for the place. The specifics of your exact problem matter.

More Analyzing When

The marriage example analyzed when but focused on *where*, the place. Let's look more at *when*, your timeframe. The person's life span or estimated life span is the equivalent of the place of Earth. Usually, we can narrow that down because we've gotten to the question we want to answer from some other piece of information. In the marriage example, identifying the oldest child, instead of just the one you descend from, is an option for narrowing the *when* of your problem. But even starting with the birth of the child you descended from narrows the timeframe down from the couple's lifespan. Doing further research to determine if you believe all the children belong to the couple, not just one of them, is also about the timeframe.

Here's another simple example. When you're starting, you might want to start researching who your great-grandparents are. That should mean you have a grandparent with a birthdate (or approximate birthdate) to provide a starting date. The parents of your known grandparent were alive nine months before your grandparent was born. If you want to identify the mother, she was alive at the time of birth. You can *estimate* the parent you want to find should have been born about twenty years or more before that date. That gives you a *timeframe*. It's a starting timeframe based on one known date.

If you have more information to create a better timeframe, that's what you should do. Asking yourself what the timeframe is **and if you can narrow it down** is analyzing your problem. Once again, you aren't ready to work on that problem if you don't have any timeframe. Basic analysis using the W-frame System can provide a tip-off that you're rushing your research by highlighting what you're missing.

Although these examples are very basic, sometimes even experienced researchers get excited and rush ahead. When you're stuck, double check you can create a good W-frame definition for your project. This simple step helps you realize you skipped doing basic background research.

Sometimes a genealogist doesn't answer one of the W-frame questions because they realize they can only estimate a date or place, and it's likely the desired information will not fall into the most likely estimate. For example, for a marriage date, you may not be sure all a couple's children belong to both of them. You still answer all four W-frame questions with your best estimate. If you don't solve your problem, reanalyze the problem using the information you just learned and create your next best estimate.

No matter your situation, you should answer all four W-frame questions. You always need a firm *who* and *what,* but it's never a problem if you have to estimate the *when* and *where.* Also, always be willing to ask yourself if your estimates are too broad. If they're too broad, back up and do additional research that will lead to better estimates. Answering all four W-frame questions is not an automatic green light that you've done everything you need to do. Not answering them is an automatic red light to stop. If you feel you can create better estimates with a bit of simple research, do it! You are focusing on that related research, and then you will focus on your original problem.

Several types of analysis exist in genealogy. Answering who, what, when, and where is the absolute most basic analysis every project needs to start with. Now, let's look at some W-frame examples. Then try creating your own W-frame analyzed problem definitions.

***

Examples

Here are a few problems Jenni is trying to solve:

- Who is the father of Henry Alford?
- When and where did Franklin Timothy Jones die?

- Who are the parents of Albert David *Hockë*?

All these have a who and a what, but none have a when or where. Additionally, finding both parents of Albert *Hockë* is two problems. Jenni has already tried to solve this, and she couldn't find a simple document that listed his parents, so she now needs to consider that finding his father is one problem and finding his mother is another. She might still find the names of both parents when trying this approach, but it's time to focus, not try everything at once!

Here are W-frame definitions for these problems.

W-frame Example #1

> Who is the father of Henry Alford, born 10 December 1850 in Alabama and died 11 May 1913 in Geneva County, Alabama?

This example uses the broad timeframe of a lifespan. Sometimes this is where you need to start when you're stuck. With the previous question, just asking who the father is, all Jenni knew she could try was searching Henry's name or learn about how to find a father. Now she knows the problem is located solely in Alabama. She can narrow her search to Alabama or learn about researching in Alabama. This is a much more actionable situation.

The birth takes place in the middle of the 19th-century with the possibility of using some early 20th-century records for Henry. If Jenni needed to learn about solving this type of problem, it would be much different working in the mid to late 19th-century than solving a problem from the 17th-century, late 20th-century, or even the early 19th-century. Just adding when and where makes such a difference!

Although it might seem obvious that these details belong with this problem, the point of the W-frame System is to make you focus. Jenni needed to stop thinking the problem was finding a father and recognize the details that make finding Henry's father different from finding someone else's father. Use a well-crafted project definition to focus on the exact problem you intend to solve. Keep refining that definition as needed.

W-frame Example #2

> Determine if Franklin Timothy Jones (born 1894 in MS), husband of Elizabeth Greeson, is the same as Frank T. Jones, that died in New York City on 22 December 1932. Family members say these are the same man. Franklin abandoned Liza and disappeared before the 1930 census.

Jenni decided to focus on whether this is one or two people rather than focusing on Franklin's, her ancestor's, date and place of death. Either option is an acceptable way to focus on this problem. You have to decide what research you would rather pursue first, as the research would differ. The way Jenni defined this problem with the W-frame System, she wants to learn about the man that died in New York City to see if that information matches what she knows about her ancestor. The research will focus on "Frank." Originally she asked, "When and where did Franklin Timothy Jones die?" which means researching "Franklin." She got stuck researching Franklin, so she did analyze her who to craft her W-frame definition.

W-frame Example #3

> Who is the father of William David Hockë, born in Kentucky in 1858 and died in Arizona in 1907. He married and lived in Cincinnati until moving out west around 1900. He hasn't been found in census records prior to 1900. The spelling of his surname is unclear, though.

This is another basic example that brings in when and where. Jenni has recognized that issues with the spelling of the surname may play an important role in this problem, so she's highlighted that in her project definition, which involves imprecise dates and places.

Staying focused can mean honing in on a date and place, like in the first example. It can also mean staying focused on the real problem you want to solve. In the third example, the problem is finding the father instead of being sidetracked by the mother, the spelling of the surname, or improving other details.

Sometimes staying focused means staying attentive to your chosen problem but shifting as needed. In this example, you might want to switch to focus on finding additional records under other spellings of this surname because the known information is sparse. The third example is an initial W-frame definition that could be altered in various ways as research continued.

Every genealogist must learn to decide what research to focus on. The point is not to solely focus on one problem. The goal is to avoid being sidetracked. The second example shows the effects of how a question about a death date could shift into a question of identity. Are two men the same person? Questions of identity allow you to analyze your who and decide which (potential) person to research first. Being focused doesn't mean only researching Franklin's death; researching who Frank is provides an equally valid alternative. With the third example, you want to know your final goal is finding the father but recognizing a troublesome surname is involved might change how you choose to approach the problem.

Here are a few other examples from other genealogists' research.

W-frame Example #4

> Who are the parents of Raffaele "Ralph" Desiderio (b. abt 1870 Salerno, Italy–d. 9 Apr 1952 Branford, CT)? Raffaele immigrated to Branford from Scafati, Salerno, Italy in 1912.

The initial question would have been, "Who are the parents of Ralph?" When considering the W-frame questions, it becomes obvious to this researcher that no research had been performed in sources that might list both parents. In this case, the W-frame definition did not specify one relationship, mother or father. This is based on the researcher's experience— knowing basic records exist for the time and place which were not used. After some basic research, if the problem isn't solved, this definition will need to be refined to focus on either Ralph's mother or father.

Your W-frame definition is unique to you and your problem. Many definitions will look similar to this one, but you need to recognize if researching for both parents simultaneously is reasonable for your situation. You need to consider if the dates and places you have are sufficient to allow you to continue researching based on what you've previously done. Analyzing a problem is all about thinking. Popping these details into an online search form frees you from doing much thinking. That may be why you are stuck. Think about your specific problem as you create your W-frame definition.

Below is a refinement of a problem about Ralph's wife. It started with the problem "Who is Michela Giordano's mother?" but then switched to example five and finally settled on the definition in example six. Both of these are good examples of W-frame definitions, so they're both included. Once you have enough experience, you might realize you need to shift your thinking, as in example six.

W-frame Example #5

What is the name of Michela (Giordano) Desiderio's mother? Michela was born in Italy about 1873, immigrated from Scafati, Italy, to Branford, CT, in 1912 with her husband and children, and died in the area in 1949. Her father's name was Geatano Giordano, and he lived in Scafati in 1912.

The above example is a W-frame definition. It meets all the requirements. But the example below is the project selected.

W-frame Example #6

Who is "Gaetano Giordano" father of Michela (Giordano) Desiderio (abt. 1873, Italy – Dec. 1949 New Haven Co., CT). Michela came to Branford, CT, with her husband and children from Scafati, Italy. Her father was listed as Gaetano Giordano, a resident of Scafati.

This is a more advanced example where not only the *what* changed but the *who*. Any genealogist might go from looking for Michaela's mother to realizing they knew nothing about the father other than his name. Remember, part of focusing is honing in on the research that needs to be done first. You can't work on two problems simultaneously, and some research needs to be done in a certain order. Focusing on a problem helps you recognize what you don't know, as well as what you do know.

Sometimes we need to improve our problem definition to help us focus our research. You'll learn more about doing this with research planning in a future chapter. Below is how you could use additional information to improve an already good W-frame definition.

The example below breaks down the W-frame questions and answers and then brings in some additional details, so you see a definition getting refined.

W-frame Example #7

Original problem: When did Berry S. Rigdon and Mary Taylor marry?
Who: Berry S Rigdon born about 1787 SC and died about 1876 Irwin County, Ga. Mary Taylor born about 1805 in Montgomery or Appling County, Ga and died before 1870 in Irwin County, Ga.
What (event): Berry and Mary's marriage
When: Before 1850 since she is with him in that census.
Where: Berry was living in Appling County 1830, 1840, and 1850 census. So they were married in Appling County or an adjacent county.

W-frame Definition Option 7a

When did Berry S. Rigdon (c. 1787 SC to c. 1876 Irwin Co., GA) marry Mary Taylor (c. 1805 GA– before 1870)? They likely married in Appling County, Georgia, before the 1850 census was enumerated.

This is a sound W-frame definition. But in this example, we will look at a few more details about this couple to further focus research.

Additional information would come from your past research, and you should cite your sources. This example excludes sources to keep it short for clarity:

> A local history states Berry came to Georgia about 1822 after his first wife died. However, in the 1830 Appling County, Ga U.S. federal census entry for B S Rigdon, there is one adult male between the ages of 40-49 and one adult female between the ages of 40-49.
> In the 1840 Appling County, Ga, U.S. federal census, there is one adult male between the ages of 40-49 and one adult female between the ages of 30-39. This age range corresponds with Mary's year of birth. In the 1850 Appling County, Ga, U.S. federal census, Berry is listed as being 63, and Mary is 45.

Now it's time for basic analysis.

Mary is considerably younger than Berry, so we should consider approximately what year she could have first married. For simplicity, you can use 20 as the age of marriage for men or women. That would be about 1825 for Mary's first marriage. It's important to know you are determining this estimate based on math since either party could be younger or older. Don't forget, in this case, you are starting with an estimated year of birth, as well. The bride, in particular, might be younger and the groom older. Twenty is a good estimate to use because it is easy to calculate in your head and allows for a younger bride or slightly older groom. We can use age 20 as an estimate, but you don't want to get that assumption confused with information from a source. Cite your sources and explain things in complete sentences to avoid confusing yourself.

The other information indicates Berry may have been married to someone else in 1830; at least, it doesn't appear Mary was his wife at that time. Supposedly he was married before, but the first wife allegedly died before 1822. Whether the woman in the 1830 census household is the first wife, an unknown second wife, or not his wife at all is immaterial to the current problem you're focusing on. Writing down your project definition can also help keep you from getting sidetracked onto other projects that don't directly serve the problem you want to work on. Mary was likely Berry's wife by 1840 but not in 1830.

If you continue to be stumped after trying the option below, consider if researching the 1830 woman is important.

W-frame Definition Option 7b

When did Berry S. Rigdon (c. 1787 SC to c. 1876 Irwin Co., GA) marry Mary Taylor (c. 1805 GA– before 1870)? They likely married between when the 1830 and 1840 U.S. federal census was enumerated. Mary could have had a previous marriage, as Berry supposedly did. This means the name of the bride might not be "Taylor." The marriage likely took place in the area around Appling County, Georgia, as Mary was a native of the area, and Berry lived there as early as 1830.

The above definition reminds you that you are interested in a narrow span of years and location. However, you don't know much about Mary's life prior to her marriage. Remember, you estimated Mary could have potentially married in 1825 or even a little earlier. She might not have a previous marriage, but it is an option your project definition could focus on.

Your Turn

Now try creating your own W-frame Definition for a problem (or several) you are stuck on. Don't worry if you can only create the most basic W-frame definition. It will still help you focus. If you can either hone in on your *when* and *where* or even do more analysis to tweak the *who* and *what*, great. But a basic W-frame definition is better than no definition.

Think about how easy it is for you to answer all four questions with as much detail as you believe your past research would allow. In other words, do you think you can better refine some of your answers, but you're struggling to find the details? This could mean you are disorganized, but it at least indicates you have additional research you want to get familiar with before doing more research on this problem.

Don't forget the fifth W; write down your definition.

Chapter 2:
Essential #1

Now that Virginia had defined the various problems she was trying to solve, she and Imogene met again to start looking at one specific problem. Gene suggested they start with Jenni's great-grandfather Henry Alford.

Jenni's problem:

> Who is the father of Henry Alford, born 10 December 1850 in Alabama and died 11 May 1913 in Geneva County, Alabama?

"OK, Jenni, let's see what you have on Henry," said Gene. Gene had asked Jenni to have any of her research on Henry ready so they could look at it. Jenni pulled up her family tree on the monitor and pushed the mouse over to Gene. Gene clicked around a bit, looking at the records Jenni had attached.

Gene returned the mouse to Jenni and asked, "How about your notes and log? Can I see those?"

Jenni looked puzzled. "Well, that's everything," she nodded at the online tree Gene had just looked at. "You see the notes I added to the events."

Now it was Gene's turn to look puzzled. "Jenni, where are the other records? This note is about the homestead file, but you don't have a homestead file attached to this tree. Where did you learn about that?"

"Huh. I don't know. I had forgotten about that."

"So you must have some notes or maybe files somewhere? What about your research log?"

"What's a research log?"

Gene was afraid that's what Jenni would say, so she patiently replied, "I'll explain about the log in a moment. What about your other files?"

"Well, that's it. I don't have files or other notes. I just added notes to the tree and attached records to it. I guess I should have saved that homestead file somehow. I don't remember where I saw it now."

"OK, I have several questions about the research you did on this Alford family, but first, I think we need to talk about tracking your research. There's no point in discussing the actual research until you've got a place to keep track of it."

In the next section, learn about what Gene and Jenni discussed regarding research tracking so that Jenni wouldn't miss parts of her past research ever again.

***

By keeping a genealogy research log, Jenni could have avoided the problem of not knowing where she saw that homestead file. A "research log," also called a "research calendar," is the traditional way genealogists kept track of *all* the research they performed, regardless of if they found anything to add to their family tree. A research log was a paper table where you recorded each source you used and how you used it. It was called a log because you logged all your research just like a flight log records flights made. A flight is logged even if it doesn't reach its destination. In that case, details from the log are often important in figuring out what happened. The same is true of your research log or other research tracking method.

Logging every search is essential because if you don't record every search, you won't remember what you've already done and will end up doing it again, wasting lots of time. You need to log or track many important details beyond just what source you tried and whether you found what you were looking for or not. However, in the 21st-century, a log format is not required. You still need to track the same information, but we needed the log format when we were limited to paper. Searching digital files opens up many more options than just a log.

Because of this difference, I prefer to refer to "tracking" your research. If you are familiar with the concept of keeping a research log, the same concepts apply when I talk about tracking your research. The advantage of using the word log was that it was not a common word you'd use every day. The challenge with the word is that some 21st-century genealogists think the importance was the format used to keep the notes—a tabular log. The format was never important; it was simply a way to organize a large amount of information every successful genealogist needed.

Today you can keep a paper or digital log or choose a different digital method that better suits your preferences. A little later, Gene will share her favorite (easy) way to digitally track research. First, Jenni, and you, need to understand why to keep track of research and what to keep track of. This helps you and Jenni avoid questions like, "Where's the homestead file this note refers to?"

Why Track Your Research

Gene reviewed Jenni's online tree and had questions. Jenni only used an online tree to track what she found when researching. That means she only tracked what she found, not everything she tried. Some key details about what she did find were also missed by only using an online tree.

Many of Gene's questions were because Jenni didn't have a research log or other tracker. If Gene had been able to review a complete research log, she would have found the answers. The answers to Gene's questions will shape the research Jenni needs to do. That future research could already be defined if Jenni had tracked her research. Instead, Jenni will need to remember or recreate the information she should have tracked. Sometimes "recreating" information from a log can be done from what we found, but sometimes it means repeating work we already did, which is a waste of at least a little but possibly a lot of time.

Tracking research lets you know what you did, and—here's what you don't want to forget to track—*why* you did it. Genealogy research is not just an online search. Many genealogists, even professionals, think knowing what websites they used is tracking their research. That's only part of it!

If you don't remember anything else from this chapter, I hope you recognize that you need to know not only what you did *and also why*. You'll know what information to record in your log or tracking method if you remember "not just *what* but *why*." However, figuring out what to record is wasting brain power, so I'm going to tell you the absolute minimum information to track. In each section, I'll further explain the purpose of tracking that particular information.

Getting Started

No matter the format of your tracking method, you need to be able to find it when needed. If you use paper, you need to keep a "log" (also called a research calendar). The table format of a paper log or calendar helps you find the information. If you work digitally, you have many other options for the structure of your tracker. This chapter focuses on the foundations you need first. Let's start by making sure you understand a couple of terms.

What Is a Search?

Describing what information to track can take a lot of explanation. Inconsistent genealogy terms can be the problem. I'll simplify by clarifying what "a search" is. Using the term search instead of listing several options depending on the type of source you're using will speed up your reading and make this whole process easier to understand.

All genealogy research is searching. The most common way hobbyist genealogists research today is by using an online search form. You understand that using that search form is searching. If you are reading a physical book looking for information, you are also searching for that information. How you try to find the information you want is your search. Whether you search the internet, use an index, or read information, you are searching. You can substitute the word search for each verb I just used; "search an index," "search for information," etcetera. I constantly catch myself using the word search to mean an online search which then leads to writing very long sentences with unnecessary descriptions of ways to perform an analog search. In this book, when I talk about *your search*, it is how you are using the source to find the information you want.

Hint: Here is some inspiration for other types of searches you should be performing besides just using a search form online. These are all types of searches and also types of research you should be trying:

- Browse digitized records
- Browse microfilm records
- Use an index in a book of records
- Read a book or records line-by-line
- Use a finding aid for a record
- Read records for select dates or other headers (instead of reading every line)

Tracking Each Search

Tracking research, often referred to as a log entry, is done each time you perform a different search. That means each additional use of a source is a different search. It's not the change in source that means you need to track new information; *it's the change in your search that requires a new log entry.*

If you are searching online census records, you enter one search to try to find the Jones family. If you want to find Mr. Jones's daughter-in-law's family, the Smiths, that's a different search. You know that is different research and a different search. It works the same with non-searchable sources. You might be using an index, so you first look for the Jones family. Then you decide to reuse that book and look for the Smith family in the index. Those are different searches.

People get confused when they start doing actions they don't equate with a digital search. To record the necessary tracking information, you have to recognize all the actions that are a search.

Let's say you have to read line-by-line to use a source. You can look for the Jones and Smith family at the same time. That is one search. The search is what you are looking for while reading that source line-by-line. Your search is reading line-by-line, looking for [describe what you're looking for].

Humans are much better at genealogy than computers. We can do one search looking for both Smith and Jones, and we'll also notice the information for the Kleinschmidts we're related to as we read the record. You were searching for the Smith and Jones families—that's your search—and you happened to find more. Note the extra information you found in your tracking method. The next section explains what details of this extra information to record.

Just because you're better at searching than a computer doesn't make recording what you did harder. Your log entry is for the search of reading line-by-line for the surnames Smith and Jones. What you found includes the details about the Kleinschmidts, even though that wasn't part of your search. You found that information while performing a search, just as searching U.S. census records can reveal someone in the household with a different name than you searched.

Your search can be using an index in a book to look for all entries indexed under the surname Miller. Your search could be the exact details you entered in a search form. Your search could be reading church minutes line-by-line looking for every woman with the first name Theodora. Your search could be reading the headings in a court docket looking for cases involving a Smith and a Reeder. Your search could be reading part of a court book between April 1843 and January 1845.

Don't get hung up on search meaning an online search using a form or search bar. You are doing research because you are searching for information. Track your research for each search you attempt, regardless if you find anything.

What Is a Source?

If you don't have a research background, you might be unsure if you properly understand what a genealogy source is. A source is a source of information. That means it can include all sorts of things like a website, a court document, the family Bible, an embroidered sampler, or even a person. But you must also recognize the difference between a source and a repository.

Repositories contain sources. For example, a library is a repository. It can contain many sources, such as books, microfilm, or other media. An archive is a repository. It can contain books, microfilm, original records, artifacts, and more. A relative's home can be a repository, too. It can contain a family Bible, family papers, genealogy research, and one or more relatives with the knowledge you want.

Similarly, large websites like Ancestry and FamilySearch are repositories. They are not sources. They contain many sources, thousands of sources, in fact. Some websites are a source, but many are a repository. This distinction is important when you're tracking your information because when you find something, you should not list your source as simply "Ancestry." That is part of your source but not the complete source. If you search part of a website, you are likely searching a source instead of the entire repository, so in that case, even your search needs to be more specific than just listing the website name as the source you searched.

Imagine if you were at a relative's house and you recorded for the source "Aunt Bertha's," and Aunt Bertha has been hoarding all the family documents and artifacts for years. Just seeing "Aunt Bertha's" as the source doesn't tell you what item you used. Was it Aunt Bertha, Uncle Ralph, the family Bible, a letter written by your fourth great-grandfather, or some pages printed from Ancestry by Cousin George for his 1998 school family history project?

To learn more about why it's important to distinguish a source from a repository, you can read this post: https://bit.ly/thats-not-a-source.

The following section about recording your source will provide additional resources about what information you need to record for a source. For now, remember a source is the source of information you used, and it needs to be extremely precise. If you talked to Aunt Bertha, the source is not Aunt Bertha's house, even though that's where you found her.

When the Repository Is Your Source

When you use large genealogy sites like Ancestry and FamilySearch, they are the repository where you find the source. You need to include the name of the website or repository as part of any citation to online material.

You don't know if you will find information before you perform a search, so track *exactly* the steps you take when you perform your search. Your online search might search an entire repository website. You can search a repository website, but you find information in a specific source within that repository.

When online research was first possible, genealogists referred to most websites as a source. It is still extremely common to hear genealogists refer to repository websites as sources. Thinking of them this way leads to multiple problems. The only time you should treat a known repository website as your source is when you didn't find information after searching the *whole site*. Record the repository website as your source in your tracking information in that case.

Tracking Essentials

Because teaching how to track effectively covers many details, this information is broken up into two parts—why we need information for tracking purposes (in this chapter) and why else we record certain information (in the next chapter).

Also, the items listed in this chapter are what I consider the bare minimum for tracking research. If you create a research log, these items *must* be in the log. Some additional information that can go in your log and notes or only in your notes is covered in the next chapter.

Date of Research

The research date is one of the traditional parts of a research log that digital genealogists often scrap. Recording the date is more than just a way to keep your entries in order, although that is one part of it.

When reviewing what you've already done, the order in which you did or didn't find information can make a difference. If you saw information on the Kleinschmidt family before you researched their in-laws, the Smiths, you might have a different idea about the Smiths. This might give you a good idea, and you found something helpful about the Smiths. Maybe the Kleinschmidt information misled you, though. Your search into the Smiths might incorporate "bad" information.

Reviewing and seeing the research order can help us understand whether our thinking was correct or flawed. Not understanding our past thinking can cause confusion when reviewing. This can waste time or, worse, mislead us again. Understanding how the research order affected our actions can help us make the best next decision. It's easier to capture this information while we research rather than try to recapture it later.

We also want the date of research in case sources change. Online records can be updated. You might need to search the same source again because new information has been added since you last used it. This is similar to using different editions of a book. Different editions can contain different information. When we create a formal citation for online records, we record the date, which acts like an edition of a book. You don't have to create formatted citations for your personal use, but recording the date as part of your tracking information ensures you still get this important piece of information.

The exact date of your search *might* not matter, but it is so easy to record, so just do it so you have it in the future. You won't know at the time you're researching that you'll need to know the date later.

WATCH OUT FOR: some digital options record the date automatically. Make sure the date won't auto-update to the date you open or use a file! You need to know the date the research was done.

Source

Next, we need to track what source we are searching. This needs to be as specific as possible and goes hand in hand with the following item. If you know how to create a genealogical citation, go ahead and record the citation. If you don't know how to cite genealogy sources, don't worry. A citation isn't necessary. You can learn what source details to include from this post, https://bit.ly/source-questions.

Don't get confused about the source to record when you search an entire repository website. Genealogists often search a repository website or even the whole internet. That is what you are searching, even though it is not an individual source. However, when you find something, you need to add the details to specify the source where you found the information.

This means before you search, the source you record might be a repository like "FamilySearch" or "Google." If you don't get the desired results, you don't have a specific source to list. This wasn't an issue before online research. You used a book. You searched a finding aid. You read through a roll of microfilm. You had to do the searching yourself, so what you searched was far more limited.

Always track what you did, which means recording the source you searched, even if it is a repository. When you find information, you must record the specific source where it is found.

Tip: If you keep an actual research log, it's helpful to add an entry for each item you find, even if you started by searching a repository website or the internet. This makes it very clear what the source is, not just the repository that was searched. I also include an entry for just the search if I need to describe what I didn't find as well as what I did find. Sometimes this will help you refine that search in the future, so you want some brief notes in your log that you see when you review. If you use the tracking suggestion in the next chapter, a separate entry isn't necessary.

Search

The source is what you were searching. Now you need to be explicit about how you are using the source. If you do an online search, you record *exactly* what search you entered in the form or box. Some sites have multiple search forms that search different things. You must make this clear, too. Record what word you put in which search field. You will include the name of the field in addition to the search term as well as indicate any selected options such as "sounds like," "adjacent county," or "exact search."

Here's an image of what a search form with fields looks like:

Each box for a specific piece of information is a field. In the next image, you can see selected search options for the different types of fields.

The search options vary by site and sometimes even by search form.

I prefer to use a screenshot of a search box if my search gets too complicated to describe. You can type a few searchable words if you believe you need searchable keywords in addition to the screenshot. If you are using paper, you'll just have to take the time to write out a detailed description.

You can use the description of your search to make it clear you searched a repository website even when you have results from specific sources from that site.

Nailing Your Online Search Description

Using an online search form has the computer do most of the work. The computer does what you and the person that programmed it tell it. Recording a detailed description of your online search is how you know what the computer looked for.

This is not the same as reading information while searching for something. You, as a human, will consider alternatives without needing a ticked checkbox. Companies are trying to make online searches closer to human searches, but search programmers often aren't genealogists, so this still has a long way to go.

Many variables exist in research. You, as a human, take those into account for your exact problem. Even if you had an experienced genealogist program the search form, they can't know what you will look for at 12:10 a.m. on March 3rd and why you are looking for it. You, the human, take into account "why." A programmer can't program the computer to make the same considerations you do; different humans make different considerations.

This is another reason the computer is good at easy research. Why you—a new genealogist—are making a search is much easier to guess and, therefore, program for than why an experienced genealogist would do a search for a problem that's stumped them for a decade.

It's vital to know what you told the computer to do. Whatever you entered in the search form or search box, that's what it looked for. Some exceptions exist. Some sites will automatically search for words as both singular and plural—adding an "s" to the end of a word. You may or may not be able to turn this option off. Genealogists care if a search is for "William" or "Williams," so look out for when this happens.

Major genealogy sites will perform broad searches to make sure you get plenty of results to choose from. An option representing "exact," as in exact date or exact spelling, is often provided. Sometimes you have to learn what special characters to use. For example, when searching Google, putting quotation marks around words is the equivalent of checking the unlabeled "exact" box to the right of a search field on FamilySearch.

The computer will search what you asked it to search for. In today's world, this is a combination of the search you enter and how the form is programmed to work. You don't know how the form is programmed, but as you use online search forms and record each search, you'll quickly learn enough to create great searches. Soon, having the source and the exact search you entered will tell you everything you need to know about what the computer looked for.

Almost as important, note if you entered an online search and got results different than what you asked for. Did it only give you results for "Smith," or did it also look for results for Smyth, Smithe, Smythe, and so forth? Each of these is a "sounds like" option. You will discover what sites search for singular and plural if you enter "William" and get as many results for "Williams" or vice versa. When you scroll happily (or unhappily) through pages of results hunting for what's relevant but don't make any notes, you often won't learn the quirks of the sites you use.

Tip: Remember, genealogy records can contain errors, such as Smith getting read by the computer as Smth. If you saw Smth as a surname, you'd automatically consider that as an option for Smith. If you tell the computer to *only* look for S-M-I-T-H, it won't give you results it reads as S-M-T-H. If you get too few results, learn ways to search to get more results without too many. For example, on Ancestry, you can use a question mark to represent one character and an asterisk to represent zero or more characters. Searching *exactly* for "Sm?th" will give you Smith and Smyth but not

Smth. Searching *exactly* for "Sm*th" will give you Smith, Smyth, Smth, and Smoath.

Bonus: Recording the exact online search will help you start to think more efficiently about how you are searching. Save time by designing the search you want to perform and record it in your tracking document before you open up the online search form. This also helps avoid errors due to overexcitement about research. Genealogists love to research. It should be exciting, so avoid the inclination to rush to results by crafting and recording your search ahead of time.

Besides needing to know what the computer looked for based on the search form entry, you also need to know if you entered all the variations to find the same information. Making a small change in the search form can change the results. Sometimes you miss making a change and will inevitably need to repeat *almost* the same search again. It is very easy to skip a variation of a search.

No genealogist is perfect. That's why tracking all searches, especially in this digital age, is crucial. One of the most important features of tracking your research is understanding what you have and haven't tried. Digital tracking is a huge timesaver, as you can copy and paste nearly identical searches or easily make a clear notation of what you changed instead of listing the entire search.

Hint: For any search, online or off, where you know you'll make minor changes, consider formatting your tracking information where you list the main search and then list each minor change instead of re-listing the full search.

Searches can have many details, and the minor change can get lost if you copy and paste the whole search. You must be clear about what you searched and don't neglect to record any changes if you choose to do this.

Manual Searching

For sources without a search form or search bar, both online and offline, you still need to describe how you use that source. You should already see that filling in an online search form asks the computer to look for certain information, possibly including variations. When an online search isn't possible, you ask yourself to look for certain information, possibly including variations. You need to record the same type of details. This can be trickier because humans will naturally and automatically consider some options we must ask the computer to look for. When recording a computerized search, it's obvious that you clicked a button to include variations of the search term. I like to record my human searches as sentences. If I decide tweak what I'm looking for as I work, I can add a note to my tracking document describing the change.

What surnames did you look up in the index? Did you use a table of contents instead? Did you skip to the part of a record based on date? Did you read the headings on each page to find what you wanted? Did you read line by line? Once again, you have to know what you did so you can know if you need to try something else that is very similar or if you're done with that source for that problem. I have even made notes to myself about having trouble reading the handwriting or being tired and thinking I might have missed seeing something I was looking for. Later I can use this information to decide whether to repeat a search.

Take a look at the examples from Gene and Jenni in the next chapter to see specific examples for different types of sources. Quickly recording a non-digital search takes practice. Sometimes the experience of not recording enough detail you need later is what will help you improve. Remember, no genealogist is perfect. Do your best.

Describing a non-digital search is not the most *obvious* information to track. That doesn't mean you should skip it. It is impossible to add the search later if you don't track it at the time. Recording your search should not be hard, but it likely needs practice. You want to focus on progress over perfection in genealogy, especially when logging your search in your tracking document.

Summary of Results

You need to know what the results of your specific search were. With a log, you need a summary because space isn't available for longer details. The tabular format makes it a log, regardless of whether it is paper or digital. Gene had questions about what Jenni had done when she reviewed Jenni's past research. Reviewing is something you should do regularly for your own genealogy problems, and the summary of your results is crucial to your review.

Your summary might be concise if you found what you were looking for. Your summary might be, "found the tombstone, see..." with the details of where you recorded the details.

Your summary might be concise if you did not find any results at all—"did not find [your search] in the index" or "no results for this search." Be careful when recording what you did not find. When genealogists rush, they equate finding results for the wrong person with not getting results. But later, you may have more information that allows you to recognize that it isn't the wrong person or maybe it's the wrong person but the father, son, or cousin with the same name.

If you get results but don't think they are the person you want, and you don't have more to say about these results, you should record something like, "got results for [name, surname, or something brief] but don't think these results are for my person." This will remind you to try this source again if you later realize you've probably overlooked relevant results.

Finding what you were looking for, as in finding the surname you were looking for, for what you think is the wrong person is different than not finding that name at all. Unless that source changed, the same search will still not contain that surname, no matter what you've learned. Make sure you are clear about getting no results versus getting no *relevant* results.

It's beneficial to indicate if you got a partial result, too. For example, you might have searched for John Smith but only found other given names with the surname Smith. In the future, you will care if a source contains the full name John Smith, J. Smith, Bert Smith, John Smythe, Johann Smithe, no "Smith," or no variations of Smith. It is your choice how much detail you record about irrelevant results, but you at least want a clear summary, even if you don't record full details.

Much like describing your human search, describing the results can be more complicated if you found some information but not a specific answer. You might get search results like Johann Smithe or J. Smythe instead of John Smith. At the time, these might seem irrelevant to your problem. When you review in the future, you might have additional knowledge that makes you realize a piece of information is a vital clue or what appeared to be a useless search result is for your person. Deciding how much information to record is a skill you have to hone.

The summary should help you know whether to pull reports, notes, or copies when reviewing your problem. It may also help you realize you should perform that search again to look at a result even if it wasn't the focus of your initial search. Once again, learning to record a summary that does this takes practice. Do your best.

Understanding how you will use this summary should help you create a useful summary. Recording "no results" should mean you literally did not find what you were looking for, not that it produced results you didn't think were what you wanted. I recommend against the brief "no results" as your entry because your future self will wonder if you are correct— the search produced no results of any type—or if you meant "no results I recognize at this time as being related to this problem."

An example from the author:

My early research logs—from offline research before online research was available—are full of "no results" as the complete summary of my findings. Those entries are essentially useless because I don't know if the surname wasn't listed or if I didn't think they were the person or family I was looking for. Simply recording "no results" means I need to repeat all that work to be sure I've exhausted that source. Many of those sources still don't have an online equivalent, so I can't just hop on my computer in my bunny slippers and knock it all out in an hour.

I have several decades more experience and knowledge at this point. Some of my "no results" likely contain results for someone I now know is relevant to my research. But I can't tell if no Pattersons were in that record, meaning I don't need to look for Pattersons again, or if I didn't recognize the Pattersons listed, meaning I should check that source again. I need to redo any research with a "no results" summary unless I'm confident that the entire source is irrelevant.

Your tracked information helps you determine if you should or shouldn't reuse a source. The summary of your findings and the description of your search are the two most important pieces you're tracking.

Make sure the summary of your search is explicit and contains enough details. The summary shouldn't be blank for any research done. It's vital to know the difference between "no results," "forgot the link," or "haven't finished the research." An empty summary means no research was performed.

Tracking and Cross-indexing

Genealogists often used a traditional paper log as a cross-index. If you are using paper, this is a very important log feature. Many genealogical items you create or save could be filed under different topics. "Topics" are whatever you use as your file names, for example, a surname, the name of the head of the family unit, or a project name. When used as a cross-index, your log is the item you use to find any research you did. Therefore, it lets you know you filed your notes under Smith, but they are the notes that also contain results for the Jones family. When using paper, if you don't use your log as a cross-index, create a separate cross-index in addition to keeping a log.

Your tracking method, both paper and digital, should point you to your related material. This includes notes, copies of documents, or even other items like maps, charts, timelines, or reports. With a digital tracking system, a separate cross-index is rarely needed. You can search for what you need and create shortcuts or links using digital file folders where an item can be filed in multiple folders.

Digital options don't necessarily mimic paper organizing. You have many options if you work digitally. Using your tracking method, you need to find—at the least—the notes you create and copies you saved. This can be part of your results summary or a separate part of your tracking method.

In the suggestion in the next chapter, you'll see your notes are with your tracking method, so you then just need to find your copies.

Your tracking method should allow you to find relevant notes and copies. It can also point to any related document. How this works depends on your tracking method and how you organize your notes and copies. It can be straight-forward by alerting you to the existence of notes and copies, which you will know how to find. It can be more involved if you use paper or prefer to use links or list file locations. Your tracking method should keep you from losing your notes and copies when reality gets in the way of perfectly organized genealogy.

Recap:

Track five pieces of information for each search you make:

- Date—You need the date to know your research order and if you need to search an updated source again.
- Source—You need to know the exact source you used.
- Search—You need to know *exactly* how you searched or used the source.
- Results—You need to know the results and summarize them.
- Cross-index—You need any additional information to find the related notes, copies, etcetera.

Chapter 3:
Dually Noted? Once Will Be Fine

"Gene, let me make sure I understand what you're telling me." Gene nodded for Jenni to proceed. "I'm supposed to write down all the research I do. Even if I just stick a name in a search form? I need all the details of what I did and what I found, even if I didn't find anything?"

"That's it!"

Jenni thought for a moment. "I see how keeping track of what I did would help me when I find something, like when I found that homestead record that I can't find now. But I'm not quite clear on why I need to know what I didn't find. How can that help me?"

"Well, at the simplest, if you don't know what you've already done, how will you know *not* to do it again? But also, maybe you do need to do it again. Sometimes we intentionally repeat research because something has changed. Online records do get updated. But even with records that don't change, what about when you learn your great-grandfather's nickname was Bud? You were searching for Dennis. Bud isn't even remotely similar. You probably didn't notice any records for Bud. Don't you want to know which records you already thought were a good idea to use and use them again with that new information?"

"Yeah. That makes sense. I had no idea the names Ann and Nancy were interchangeable in the past. I could not find a great-grandmother in any records. I thought she had my ancestor and died. Turned out I just needed to look for records for Nancy, not Ann. Then I found she was the only wife of my great-grandfather. I have wanted to go back and look for her in some of those records again, but I'm not sure what I looked at. I guess I have to start from scratch. That seems kind of silly now that I know there's a faster way."

"Exactly. Research tracking makes a huge difference. What everyone finds hard is deciding what format works best for them. Keeping a research log on paper was hard. Tons of forms were available, but the spaces were so tiny you couldn't fit all the information in. Now you can pick a digital option you like, and you'll have the space you need, *and* it'll be searchable."

"That sounds much better."

"It is. Just make sure you do it every time. That's the hardest part."

"Can't I just save something from my computer's browser to make this easier?"

"You can copy and paste, but not all research happens online. But even when it does, your browser history is just a date and part of your search description. A web address won't tell you the source when you review your notes. It'll just be a web address. The site title that appears often isn't the individual source you used. Or it's so truncated it's not helpful. And then there's your exact search and summary. They don't appear in your browser history at all. And I haven't even told you about one of the absolute key elements that went in a traditional log, but I keep it in my notes. There's no way saving information from your search history will record it."

Jenni looked a bit overwhelmed as Gene had gotten increasingly excited about telling her why her browser history was a terrible substitute for a research log. Gene took a breath and explained what was a better option, "I find it a waste of time to visit my browser history unless I just forgot to record a search. It's faster to copy and paste from the actual page you are using or even take a screenshot of your search. The image won't be searchable, but you don't always need to search the text of your search. Screenshots can save a lot of time when used correctly."

Jenni was now nodding along with Gene, so Gene continued, "All this information was traditionally kept in your research log, but I keep it in my notes. In fact, I want to show you a faster digital way to start tracking all your research. If you take digital notes, you can use them instead of another tracking method. There's just one thing you have to be careful to do."

In the next section, learn the one thing you must do, plus how Gene's faster way to start digitally tracking research works, no log needed.

✳✳✳

Gene recommended that Jenni start tracking her research by keeping the tracking information in her digital genealogy notes.

When genealogists used paper, certain information needed to be recorded in both the log and the notes because we couldn't search our notes. Genealogists needed to see certain details when reviewing the paper research log. But that's not an issue with digital methods.

For genealogists who have never (successfully) kept a research log or other tracking method, taking digital notes can be a much easier way to start. This reduces the work that has to be done without skimping on any of the information. If you later want to create a separate log or tracker, you can copy and paste the relevant details from your notes to your log. In fact, it can always be easiest to start by creating digital notes and then copy and paste information from the notes to the tracking method, should you want a separate digital tracking method.

Moving information from your notes to a log or tracker can be automated if you are familiar with automation options. We won't go over ways to automate because many options are available. How you automate is a purely personal choice. Instead, we'll focus on how to take great genealogy notes.

First, let's review what goes in the most basic research log:

- You need the date you did the research.
- You need to know the source you used.
- You need to know exactly how you searched the source.

- You need to know the results and have them summarized.
- You need any additional information to find the related notes, copies, etcetera.

Most of this information also belongs in your notes, except for your results summary.

Digital notes should include the same information as a research log, plus more. Remember, if you use paper, you need a separate log because it's how you find your non-searchable notes. Your notes should always contain the same information as your log, whether digital or paper. That means if you take digital notes (good notes, that is), it's safe to only take notes because you haven't forgotten to record any information.

If you decide to track digitally using your notes, here's the one thing you absolutely must do...

You must create notes for ***every*** source you use.

If you don't use a separate tracking method, and if you don't create notes, you have not tracked the research you attempted. What's essential about the research log concept is not the format but tracking every search you attempt, regardless of the outcome.

Here's an example of how this affects your actual research. I have kept an Excel research log for years. I love Excel and how I can search, sort, and filter my log to help me review past work. I use Excel because I love spreadsheets and use some of the more advanced features. So how does keeping an actual log affect my research sessions?

I create my log entry first, and if I find information, or need to make longer notes, then I create a digital notes document. I'll include the name of the notes file in my log entry, and if I'm on my primary computer at home, I make that filename a link to the notes.

So, when keeping an actual log, I create the log entry first and only create a notes document if I need it. If you decide to use your notes as your tracking method, you must create a notes document before you get started. In a later chapter, you will learn another shortcut that makes this even easier. It's vital that you understand the importance of creating notes before you start researching if they are your tracking method.

This book is not about doing perfect genealogy. Perfect doesn't happen. It takes practice to do great genealogy. The less time you have—the more of an Occasional Genealogist you are—the more you need to be prepared for less-than-ideal situations. It can be hard to find time to get enough practice to do great genealogy when you're an Occasional Genealogist. I know I need every shortcut I can get because I have so little time for my own research. Even when I do have some time, I often get interrupted.

When time is not on your side, what you *can* do is understand your options and if they are bad, good, better, or best. The shortcut in a later chapter is a "best" option. But if you find yourself in a research situation where you just don't have time for that whole shortcut, starting your tracking entry—which may be your notes—before you start researching is a "better" option. In some situations, you don't need the full shortcut, which means starting your notes before you start to research is the "best" option. This situation is briefly discussed in section three.

Starting digital notes before you start researching is such a great option that I'm considering switching to that approach the next time I find time for my own research. I already use the shortcut, which you'll learn soon, for client work which is why I know it's such a time-saver! The problem is that I love my Excel log and want to use it. But trying to keep an Excel log on an iPad, Chromebook, or, heaven forbid, a smartphone is a roadblock that stops me from researching. On those devices, taking notes is much easier than filling in a spreadsheet. I know the reality is that I will likely not update my Excel log, and I'll lose all the advantages of having it.

Tracking your research does not help if you only track random research sessions. To get the full advantages of tracking, you need to be consistent. That means finding what works for you. Until you figure this out, taking notes every time you research is an option that captures all the information you need.

Here's a quick reminder of why you want to track every search you perform:

- If you searched for every variation of the information you can think of, and the source couldn't have been updated, you don't need to search that source again.
- If you've learned something new or the source contains new information, you *do* want to search the source again.

Another reason is that you can use "negative evidence," which is when you have learned something because you did *not* find what you were looking for. For example, when a person does not appear on a tax list or the accompanying defaulters' list, it means they did not legally have to pay taxes. You can check the laws to see what this includes. Reasons for this exclusion might be that they didn't live there, they didn't own land there, they were too old, they were too young, they were female, they weren't a white male, or various other reasons. Combined with other information you know, not finding someone on a tax list can be helpful.

Using negative evidence is tricky because all relevant records need to exist. If you had a tax list but not the defaulters' list that goes with it, your person might be on the defaulters' list, which means they didn't pay their taxes, not they legally didn't have to.

Before using negative evidence, you would also track what records you tried to find that didn't exist. Records you discover that don't exist are great items to include in notes since they may not fit neatly into your log. However, if you use a log, you would need to figure out how to record the non-existent records in your log or otherwise adjust your process so you consider them when reviewing and planning future research.

If you don't record every search you make, including searching if a record exists, you waste time in the future and potentially miss out on information that can help you. Genealogists track their research so they can use that information. Notes have always been a great place to keep these details.

When paper was the only option, we needed a log to help us find our relevant notes. Imagine having a four-drawer filing cabinet full of notes. You wouldn't flip through everything in it whenever you wanted to review a project. Sure, you might be able to pull a couple of file folders, but likely other material you need is filed under a different topic. Your log helped you find that. If your project involved a whole drawer of notes, the log was a quicker way to review what you'd find in all those files. In contrast, today, you can digitally search to find your digital notes.

You still need the same things as in the paper age, but you can achieve them differently. You still need to track everything to save time. This helps you avoid repeated work and gives you clues from what you don't find or even negative evidence. You still need to find your relevant notes and *quickly* review them. For some genealogists, this means you still need to keep a log. You will need to find the right tracking solution or note retrieval option for you. But one thing hasn't changed, you still need notes. Digital notes are a safe place where anyone can start tracking all their research.

So you've been reminded of what goes in a log or tracker and why you need to track every search. But why do you even need genealogy notes in the 21st-century? Couldn't you keep just a log?

Why Notes

In the 21st-century, genealogists often don't take notes because recording facts you can attach to your family tree seems redundant. And it is. But your notes need to contain much more than just facts. You don't have to record the facts if you capture them somewhere else. You can simply refer to that location. This choice is up to you. There should be so much more to your notes than "just the facts."

> **Hint:** When deciding if you need to record the facts in your notes, what you want to consider isn't just how fast you can create your notes. You need to consider reviewing your research in the future and how long that will take. When creating a process for yourself, stop and go through the whole process before doing too much research so you have a chance to make adjustments. Make sure the system you're setting up is something you can and will use.

Keeping notes and attaching information to a tree is no different than in the past when you made a photocopy of a document because so much of it was important. You still wanted notes, but you could reference the copy if you needed to see the actual document. Photocopies, digital or paper, don't replace notes.

Genealogical notes are much better than image copies for two reasons. First, notes capture clues and ideas. Copies of records or entries in a family tree can't capture either of these. Second, notes are faster to review than copies. Notes are not faster to review than a family tree, but a review of your family tree is incomplete. It misses the clues and ideas you need to review. Notes hit the sweet spot between being quick to review while still containing all the information needed.

The earlier chapter on research tracking talked about reviewing your tracking information. So which is it? Do you review your tracking method or your notes? If you keep a separate tracking method, such as a research log, review it first because that's faster than reviewing all your notes. Your tracking method is a summary that helps you decide which notes to review for the exact problem you are working on.

A review hierarchy exists, and we'll cover that by the end of this book. For now, you've learned why you need to track certain information, and now you're learning what to capture in your genealogy notes. You must take notes before creating the rest of the hierarchy, so we can't cover those options yet.

So why are genealogy notes so crucial to create? Most importantly, they capture clues, even clues you may not recognize as clues at the time. Clues can be a clue to an answer or a clue to another source that exists. They can be clues to something that happened to our ancestors. Most of what we find in a source are clues. They suggest something but don't prove it. When we take notes, including all the items listed in the following section, we often capture clues we don't recognize as clues. We also get a chance to point out what we think is a clue. Reviewing our notes gives us another opportunity to recognize clues, combine them, or use them in a new way. Clues are like building blocks; we can use them in different ways at different times. Clues are captured in our notes.

Notes are also a place to record ideas. You will lose most of your ideas if you don't record them. You will come up with important ideas while researching that you won't think of any other time. You won't have the same ideas when you review your notes or even review the entire source. This is partly why we record the date in our tracking information. Your ideas depend on what just happened, such as what source you looked at before or what you reviewed before doing new research. Your ideas rely on past research. Later, you may know something new or be distracted by a red herring (a false clue). You want to capture ideas when you have them. You can't be sure if an idea is really good or really silly, so record all your ideas in your notes.

Remember, you need clues and ideas which a photocopy or family tree doesn't contain. Reviewing your notes is also faster than reviewing a photocopy. Yes, you may want to review photocopies sometimes. Most of the time when you review, and you should review a lot, you don't need to look at a copy of a document. Reviewing your notes is enough in most cases. If you need to look at document copies every time you review, either your notes are incomplete, or you aren't reviewing enough!

> **About that earlier hint**: I suggested you needed to test whether it's faster to include "facts" in your notes or just someplace like your tree or software. Part of this is recognizing that you don't need every single detail in your notes. You can save a photocopy just as full fact details can be saved to your online tree. Ideally, you *include enough facts* in your notes to allow for a sufficient review. You can always refer to your tree, software, or a copy of the record if you need more information. You'll make the best use of your time by reviewing your notes in most situations,

referring to other documents only sometimes. I can't give you specific directions on what pieces of information go in your notes and what goes in your tree to do this. It'll vary dramatically by the research you're doing. You need to learn from experience. That means researching and reviewing!

The following sections show the *minimum* information you want to record in your notes.

If you're new to taking notes, especially if you're not familiar with how to "evaluate your sources," make sure to grab the free bonus material for more resources: https://genealogyskills.com/bonus/.

I'll explain note-taking as if you're taking digital notes and *not* keeping a separate tracker. You could make some alterations to this process if you use paper, but explaining all the options can be confusing. This process will create great notes regardless of whether you use paper or digital and whether you keep a separate tracking method or not. In other words, this is a safe process to follow in any scenario, although if you keep a separate tracker or are using paper, it might not be the fastest option.

Start taking notes *before* you perform a search or open a source to look at. Although you can get this information once you begin the actual research, there's so much temptation to plunge ahead to review what you found. Starting your notes before you perform a search reduces the temptation to skip recording this important information. If you find valuable results, you won't want to stop and record the initial information after your search. Set yourself up for success by starting your notes before you search.

Before You Search

Date

First, your notes need to be dated. Start new notes on a new day, even if you are continuing research. Remember, you need to review. Notes that run on and on are harder to review. Creating new notes on a new day gives you a natural break when you create long notes. You also need to date your notes for the same reasons you record the date when you track research.

If you decide you have a good reason *not* to start a new note file on a new day, make sure you record the date within your notes document. Appropriate scenarios for this tweak usually happen because using the source is very slow, such as reading bad handwriting line by line in a very large book, like court records or church records. It might be important to read line-by-line, but you might not have anything to record. Nonetheless, you've had a break in your thinking, so listing the new date can help you understand why you did something when you review it in the future.

Source

Next, you need to know what source you are using. This is like recording the source for tracking purposes. Your notes might include multiple sources, or you might prefer to create a unique set of notes for each source. This personal choice relates to your process—how you like to review, what works best for you, and your available time.

If you aren't already familiar with the source details you need for a citation, there's a resource in the bonus material to help you. Sign-up at: https://genealogyskills.com/bonus/

A Trick for Checking Source Details

Most of us learned about citing sources when we were in school. Thinking back to this experience can help you if you didn't continue to develop your source citing skills into college or beyond. Genealogists need to be far more precise in their citations than what most people learned. But if you don't know much about citing sources, grasping the basics will make tracking your research easier.

I know I misunderstood citing sources, as taught for those early research papers. I thought the point was so the teacher knew you didn't cheat and make up the information. I thought we were taught to cite sources so someone else could find and verify the information. This is true in genealogy, but I like to think of that as a secondary reason.

One of the quirks you might find for genealogical citation, versus other citation experiences, is genealogists need a great deal of citation detail to judge the quality of the research. You need this in your own research for yourself just as much as for someone else.

So, to make it easier to remember how much detail you need to record, you need to know that first, you need enough details to judge the quality of your own work, and so someone else can judge the quality of your work. This isn't about being judgmental; it's so you can deal with your questions as you continue to research. I consider this the primary reason genealogists cite their sources.

Second, you need to record the details of the source so you or someone else can find that exact source again. I always had it impressed on me, until I was becoming a professional, that this was the primary reason. The details to find a source again won't include everything you need to judge the quality of your source, though.

Mentally I like to remember I need details for source evaluation. Source evaluation is judging the quality of your research. I then remind myself to double-check and see if those details also include everything to find the source again. You don't have to worry about what you need for source evaluation details if you use the notes template from the bonus material. The details requested include source evaluation information.

When you are getting started, you may need to focus on recording details that would allow someone else to find the source you used. Starting with the details for finding a source again can help you learn to recognize a repository versus a source. Even if you aren't sure what's the source versus repository or the source title versus a collection name, recording details so someone else can find the information will capture enough information. Don't just use a URL (web address). These can change, and you'd be stuck.

Remember, you want enough detail so someone could find the source again, *even if they have to access it in a different way.* This could be on a different website or even offline in its original format. Thinking about the details you'd provide so anyone could find the source again, no matter how they need to get it, helps you capture all the details you need.

Online genealogy information almost always comes from an offline source. Genealogists need the details of the online and offline sources. You will see in the examples a source that shows the online source and the original offline source. Someone who didn't have a subscription to that website could use microfilm as the offline source. If they had access to a different website with the same offline source, they could find the same information.

Why You Are Using This Source

This item traditionally went in our research log or was how we divided up logs. *Why* never had enough room in a paper table, though. *This is one of the most important things you will record*! Many online or automated options miss recording this vital piece of information. Only a human researcher, you, knows what is in your brain when you decide to perform a search. This cannot be automated.

Describe why you have chosen to use this source. This is crucial, so don't skip it. Ask yourself, "What do I think I will find in this source," or "Why do I think I should check this source for the problem I'm working on."

Sometimes the answer is simple, "Census records are easy to use and have lots of details; I always need to check them." But if you have a specific reason for choosing a source, that's especially important to record. Here's an example.

> I found an old message board post about this Patterson family, and in it, someone said one of the daughters applied for money because they were Indian [Native American]. They didn't list the actual source, but I think this is it. These records often contain details of parents, grandparents, sisters, brothers, and even great-grandparents and aunts, and uncles. I'm looking for any applications that could be for descendants of Rolin Patterson to see what details they provide. The surname probably isn't Patterson if it is descendants of daughters.

The first census example might fit on a paper log (a log with boxes for each piece of information), but it would be hard to fit the longer second description on a paper log. Take advantage of the space in your notes to clearly explain your *why*.

Your Search

Between the *why* and the description of your search, make sure it is clear what you are looking for. Don't just record a detailed online search that doesn't explain why you are performing it. Similarly, don't list a very clear *why* but neglect to list what you searched.

Recording *why* makes "no relevant results" a helpful summary. What you search for and why defines what a relevant result is. You could make the same search with a different why and suddenly find relevant results. This can be because you learned something new or because your brain interprets the results differently when you start with a different purpose. This is even more likely with manual searches, such as reading records, but it can happen with digital searches or using an index.

Option: Background/Starting Information

Related to your why and your search, you may need details in your notes that are "background information." When using the Patterson example, your why might list each daughter's name and her basic details. You probably can't enter all those details into a search form, but later when you review your notes, you will see the starting information you had and the searches you performed. When you review, you might realize you forgot a search variation or maybe were missing some vital background information.

Details about your starting information or background information are important but can appear in various places in your notes. You can call it "background" or "reason for search" or record it under your search description. It doesn't matter; just ensure you know what you were doing and why. Later you'll learn a shortcut that makes this note-taking portion as fast as possible.

Having the why, the background, and the search description in your notes is crucial to future reviews and your future success.

Apparent Problems

If you see any problems with the source you will use before you even search, take note of them. This can be problems with a physical item, like damage to a physical book. It can also be issues you discover in a digital item.

Here's how you might discover digital issues before using the source. To gather the details for a digital source—or just because you're a good genealogist—you might read the collection or item description. It might reveal the digital item does not include the location or dates you need to search. This might mean you don't perform a search, but you should still track your use of this source. You don't want to sit down to use that source for that same date or place later if records aren't added. With digitized sources, you might want to check and see if records were added, though. This is why we track *every* source we touch, even if we decide not to search it once we learn more about it.

Another example of a problem is when a source is not as comprehensive as the description or name makes it appear. This can happen with physical or digital sources. Books of handwritten original records may have lost pages over time or might have been used for a purpose different than what was recorded on the cover. Microfilm can sometimes have a title that doesn't correctly reflect what is in the physical item that was filmed. Unlike digital collections, microfilm won't be updated, so knowing the contents don't match the title can save many repeated attempts to search that film. Normally we discover physical sources, including microfilm, are incomplete *after* we take the time to search them. We have an advantage with digital sources that have detailed descriptions *if* we first read the description before using the source.

Incomplete collections are a problem because the title and contents don't match. This is pretty common with some of the most basic online databases. Think of collections like "Georgia Marriages 1797-1899" or "English Parish Registers, 1550-1990." Digital sources with titles covering a large area and larger timeframe never include every record of that type in that timeframe. You have to look at the description to see what is included. It's a good idea to start your notes and then check the description to see what is or is not included when using a mega collection of this type. It'll save you time later to go ahead and record this information.

For sources that can't be digitally searched, it's worthwhile to quickly look at the source to see if the records appear to match the title or description before you begin your slow use of that source. You can also do this with browsable, searchable items. However, if sixty seconds of searching could provide a result, it's not as critical to first check for problems in a searchable digital source. If your search fails, then you'd check for problems, as described below.

Once You Search
Are There Any Problems?

Recording source issues in your notes is crucial. You might find them before you start or after you perform a search. Whenever you see an issue, make a note, preferably immediately. Not recording issues often results in large amounts of wasted time later, and it can be hard to remember if you found an issue after you get distracted by something else.

Problems with a source are even more likely to be found once you perform your search. Maybe the court record book looked in good shape until you got to page 352 and discovered pages 353-399 are missing, and the index indicated you need page 363 (of course).

Digital searches can reveal damage seen on an image, results that don't match what was searched, or searches that just don't appear to work correctly. Whatever problem you encounter, make a note. For some problems, you can find a workaround—search using the "keyword" field instead of the "last name" field or other field if your search just doesn't seem to work correctly. Some issues we can't work around. If page 363 was ripped out in 1852, there's no hope for finding it; you'll need to find a different source to use.

Taking notes also slows you down, so you recognize if page 363 was ripped out of the original book or if the link from page 362 to the next page just doesn't work correctly. Yes, this happens. You can find a workaround if the link is broken, but the page in the original source was scanned.

Results of Your Search

We've already touched on deciding whether to include all the facts you find in your notes or only include a reference to them. You can attach pieces of information to your online tree, but you should also note that you found what you were looking for and where you attached it. Some small details don't have a place in your tree. Record those in your notes. If you didn't get the results you wanted, make a note of it. If you have any ideas or questions that come up, also record them.

Your ideas and questions are sometimes the most valuable part of your research. They can occur at any time, so it's a good idea to be ready to take notes regardless if you're doing research, reviewing, performing analysis, or writing up your conclusion.

Example #1

Source

Your source can be a formatted citation, but it can also include just the details needed to complete the citation. Below is an example of a formatted citation followed by the free-form version you could record.

Source (formatted citation)

"U.S., Newspapers.com Marriage Index, 1800s-current," database with linked but inaccessible image, *Ancestry* (*https://www.ancestry.com* : accessed February 2023), entry for O. H. Smith to Hellen S. Anderson, abt. 1850, Vermont.

Source (free form)

U.S., Newspapers.com Marriage Index, 1800s-current, Ancestry.com

> Linked to images but requires an add'l Newspapers.com subscription, that I don't have. From the source information:
> Source Citation
> Aurora of the Valley; Publication Date: 10/ Oct/ 1850; Publication Place: Newbury, Vermont, USA; URL: https://www.newspapers.com/image/355535209/?article=f4a0f933-2952-4323-8b9f-97510adf2c30/35992850-6ee4-4c3f-9ad9-4bf0f-ba3f5dd& focus=0.6570886,0.06599655,0.80993855,0.17447089&xid=3398

- The accessed date doesn't need to be recorded in the free form source because it is the date of research you should have already recorded.
- The details about the "entry for" don't belong in the source section because they belong in the results.
- You know the URL for Ancestry is ancestry.com, but if the web address is not clear, that should be recorded as part of the source.
- The text under "Source Citation" is copied and pasted directly from the results screen. In a free-form recording of your source details, you don't need to worry about reformatting this. If you are creating a formal citation, you will likely adjust this information.

Free-form citations are much faster to create. They should contain all the details needed to create future citations of any format. There isn't one formatted citation for information. The formatted citation depends on the text the citation is for, not just what the source is. Save time in your notes and create fast, free-form citations with *all the details you might need.* Copy and paste is your friend.

Search

The easiest way to accurately record your online search is with a screenshot of the search form. Make sure to type any words you want to search for as text in your notes if needed. Here's an example that resulted in the O.H. Smith record used in the source example.

Searching: "U.S., Newspapers.com Marriage Index, 1800s-current," Ancestry.com. These details appear as the source, so they wouldn't be duplicated when recording the search.

The search form is longer, but this shows the fields used. If you enter information in other fields, make sure your screenshot reflects them.

To record this search textually, you need to make sure it is clear you used separate First and Last name fields; you searched the "Marriage" and "Any Event" years but without using the checkbox ("Exact +/-..."). If you need to add some searchable text to go with the screenshot, you can include "Harold Smith, 1850," as you have shown in the actual search. It's much easier to use a screenshot!

Results

Sticking with the example of O.H. Smith from U.S., Newspapers.com Marriage Index, 1800s-current on Ancestry. Let's imagine we didn't find what we wanted. Here's how the results would look (the search was recorded as shown in the previous section).

> Only three results with a publication date in 1850, none for a "Harold Smith." 14,549 total results. Did not skim through all of them. All other results in the first 50 are for 20th-century publication dates.

Here's how this might look if we wanted the results for O.H. Smith.

> O.H. Smith to Hellen S. Anderson, published 10 Oct 1850, Aurora of the Valley (Newbury, Vermont). Requires a subscription to Newspapers.com to see the image. From thumbnail, appears to only be a list of marriages that occurred, not a full article.

Example #2

Source

Jeannette Tillotson Acklen. *Tennessee Bible Records.*
(Part I, Part II is Tombstone Records).
[repository] DAR Library

Search and Results

There is no Rainbolt or Dugger listed in the contents. Mathes, p 291 - Mathes in Cartwright Bible record (indicating "Contents" acts as an index of sorts).
Williams-pp181, 186-7, 189, 318-323
181-Lewis and Sarah (Oslin) Williams family-Lewis 1755-1836, VA family
186-7 John (son of Lewis, supposedly) and Mary Williams family
189-Daniel (1751-1831) and Sarah (Nixon) Williams, no children listed
318-George and Rebecca (Taylor) Williams children include Pleasant m. Sarah Smith Peters (no dates for any of these)-heading says "copied from data gathered by George T. Williams, i.e. research).

This is an example of a published book used when an opportunity presented itself, not after planning research. The tracking information was tracked in an actual (digital) research log but using a concept similar to the Roll-up.

What's important to note in this example is the results changed as research was done. Before research started, it was just a list of surnames. Then when using the "Contents" (this book doesn't have an "index"), the page numbers were added. Then when each page was checked, the notes were added. It appeared nothing was helpful for the surnames of interest, but enough details were captured to know to recheck this source should it turn out they were relevant.

Example #3

Source

> Ancestry.com
> "U.S., Citizenship Case Files in Indian Territory, 1896-1897." NARA microfilm publication P2293.
> Case 124

This example also came from a digital, spreadsheet research log and includes a formatted portion which is bibliography-style. All the details for a footnote or endnote are captured but are not in the "source" cell in the log and therefore aren't shown. This type of result is often easier for less-experienced researchers to capture in notes so there's no need to worry about which cell records various source details.

Results

> follow-up on affidavits on images 16 & 18
> brief summarizing all relationships is image 10-12
> image 13 Catherine Montgomery says she is "a grand daughter of Edward Williams and a Gr.

> grand daughter of Peggy Crittendon who was a
> Cherokee indian by blood."
> where is exhibit E?

These results show follow-up tasks and a question. Images were downloaded and saved with image numbers as part of their file names for easy follow-up. The link to the images appeared in a separate cell in the log.

Example #4

Source

> Walton County, Georgia Court of Ordinary, Poor School Fund Records, 1829–1897, "Lists of Poor Children 1829–1832," RG 247-2-22, Georgia Archives, Morrow.

These are the original records, not online images or microfilm.

Results

> IMG_3174.jpg and IMG_3175.jpg (zoomed) and IMG_3176.jpg (zoomed) and IMG_3177.jpg (backside) and IMG_3178.jpg (front label)
> 249th Dist.
> 20 August 1832
> Four labeled columns, Parents, Males, Females, Ages

> John Greeson [sons] Geo. W. Greeson 10, [daughters] Nancy Greeson 11, Sally Greeson 8 James Greeson [sons] Mountain Greeson 10, Greenberry Greeson 8, [daughters] Letita Ann Greeson 12
>
> Also on this page are Knights and Barkers, a Mitchell is the trustee

These were notes taken when the images were reviewed later. This allowed the file names to be added to the results. A screenshot of the relevant portion of the images was included in the notes which made it clear what the text referred to without requiring formatting to recreate the columns. Listing the other names on the page allows these notes to be found via a search when working on a project for those surnames. It did not appear the surnames were significant at the time of review but they will easily be found if needed, later.

Examples of More Sources

The following examples are formatted citations. Remember, you don't have to format your sources. These give you ideas of the pieces of information different types of sources might need.

An Online Database (No Images)

> "Wisconsin, Death Records, 1867–1907," database, *FamilySearch* (*https://familysearch.org/ark:-/61903/1:1:XLCJ-9YK*: June 2017), Mine P. Maynard, 1901; citing FHL microfilm 1,306,212.

A Different Repository Website

> "Fairmount sexton's records, 1891-1953, Fairmount Cemetery, Denver, Colorado.," PDF document, *Denver Public Library Digital Collections* (*http://digital.denverlibrary.org/cdm/ref/collection/p16079coll14/id/3578*: accessed May 2017), pp. 464, 471, 967–8, 1217.

Microfilm Available at Different Repositories

> South Carolina. *Accounts Audited of Claims Growing out of the Revolution in South Carolina, 1775-1856*. South Carolina Department of Archives and History, Columbia. FHL microfilm 2410958. Family History Library, Salt Lake City, Utah.
> Note: SC call # S 108092, roll 119

Your Turn

Use the citation resource from the bonus material to practice creating free-form citations yourself: Sign-up at: https://genealogyskills.com/bonus/ .

Chapter 4:
This Is How You Do It

Jenni was ready to go the next time she and Gene met. But she also had a burning question.

"Gene, I figured out so much more by going back and taking notes on some of the sources I had already used but, honestly, how am I supposed to have time for this? It takes such a long time to keep a log and take notes?"

"You don't have to keep a separate research log unless you prefer that format. And even if you do, you can just copy and paste the information from your notes to your log."

"But it still takes *sooooo* much time. I'm never going to be able to remember what I did last time I worked on my problem."

"Jenni, you don't need to remember. That's why you're taking notes. You don't need to worry about James shutting off the computer each night. You're recording your progress in your notes." Gene could see the light bulb go off in Jenni's head. "Notes make genealogy easier because you don't need to remember. When you go on your cruise this summer, you can forget about family history and pick back up whenever you're ready. You can review what you've done by reading over your notes."

"OK. I get that. But…" Jenni's look of realization started to shift into a frown. "It's going to be a lot of notes. Or at least it will be a lot of notes the longer I work on this. I understand *why* I should write all these things down, but I'm going to need a lot of time to read all those notes. It just seems like the longer I work on my family history, the more time it'll take. That's fine if I have time, but I don't want to go months because I can't give up a Saturday just for genealogy."

Gene paused to think. "That's a legitimate problem, but taking a whole day to read your notes and then find more time to do your research is not your only option. I think I need to tell you about the rest of the genealogy research process. It's how genealogists have successfully solved problems for generations. Once you know all the parts, there's a shortcut my cousin taught me, so you don't need a whole day to catch up."

In the next section, learn all the steps involved in the full genealogy research process and then learn the shortcut.

***

Here's Jenni's problem. How do you have time for all this note-taking and reviewing, as well as research?

Most hobbyist genealogists have this problem. Technology can help us out, but first, we need to be familiar with the full genealogy research process so we know how to use technology to help us instead of inadvertently using it to *cheat* that process.

To be clear, I refer to something that saves you time as a "shortcut." A shortcut that will cause you problems, whether immediately or years down the road, is a "cheat." You need to find every shortcut you can. You want to avoid every cheat. With that said, some cheats are worse than others, and life happens. That means cheats happen. You want to be in control of your research. Determining if a cheat is a big or a small problem is part of this. You can't assess the impact of a cheat without understanding the genealogy research process. *Understanding* the purpose of the process, not just reciting it, is paramount for doing great genealogy.

The Traditional Research Process Explanation

Genealogy research process explanations often involve something like this five-step process:

- Analyze the problem
- Plan research
- Research
- Report
- Repeat

The five-step process is easy to remember because it is so simple. Just five steps, start at the beginning with a problem, plan your work, do the work, write about what you did, and start again. But genealogists run into a few common issues before this process is ingrained, and they follow it consistently and correctly.

This traditional process is simplified, heavy on research, and light on the things that really help genealogists with problems that take more than a day to solve. *Most* genealogy problems take more than a day to solve, so this is a huge issue.

Also, many genealogists only understand how to research, yet three other actions happen in the five-step process. Even when genealogists try to plan research, analyzing the problem and reporting often seem intimidating. Additionally, sometimes research planning can seem like a monumental task. This means most of the process is misunderstood or skipped.

Overall, the five-step process is easy to remember but surprisingly hard to implement. When it's hard to implement, it's likely to be abandoned. Even if you try to follow it, sneaky cheats can work their way into *your* process as you attempt to figure out how to follow the steps.

Revising the Traditional Explanation

I decided I wanted to explain the research process differently for the readers of my blog, *The Occasional Genealogist*. Like Jenni, they didn't want to wait months to have a whole Saturday free for genealogy. They didn't want to be perpetually stuck, either. A good research process is the way to make consistent progress, regardless if you're an Occasional Genealogist or an *often genealogist*.

A strong process is even more critical for Occasional Genealogists because they cannot rely on their memory. If they have the time, *often genealogists* will try what Jenni did, working a little on everything so they don't forget. You've already learned about context switching, and hopefully, you are starting to see that notes are a critical part of successful research. Jenni's cheat skipped the notes and was all context switching. Unfortunately, most 21st-century genealogists learn to do genealogy in this exact way.

A different, more effective explanation of the genealogy research process is needed so that Occasional Genealogists can understand, remember, and follow the process. The five-step process I mentioned at the start of the chapter isn't actually "steps." They are four phases of research (plus "repeat"). That's partly why the traditional explanation is misunderstood or over-simplified. You think you are getting instructions on what to do, but it's more complicated than it first appears.

The Brick Wall Solution Roadmap

I created a modified explanation of the research process in the Brick Wall Solution Roadmap. The idea is that this process is like a map for a road trip. It will take you from where you are today to a solution to your brick wall problem. It's important to remember that the genealogy research process is about solving a problem. It doesn't tell you how to organize your research or how you can share or present your results. It's only about solving a problem. At the end of this book, we'll quickly look at what you should do instead of the process if solving a problem isn't what you want to do with your genealogy time some days.

I've had blog readers argue that the process doesn't work, but they use scenarios that aren't about solving a problem.

For example, they might be trying to find all the census records, which is not a research problem; it's a research task. Reminding yourself all this work is about solving a problem can help you justify the time. It's why I put the phrase *brick wall* in the title of my altered explanation.

In contrast to the traditional explanation, the Brick Wall Solution Roadmap is six action steps, you follow in a specific order:

1. Define the problem
2. Review
3. Write up your results
4. Make a plan
5. Execute the plan
6. Repeat steps one and two, only refining the problem (step one) if needed

This is the same as the traditional five-step process, just expressed differently. This should seem very familiar to what Jenni learned regarding note-taking and research tracking. However, this process also allows you to plan education or organization instead of research. You might have an idea or question you need to address before doing more research, and the six steps aren't altered if that's the case.

Genealogists need to do other things besides research to do great genealogy. The best way to accomplish those things is to make a plan. When you need to research, the Roadmap is the genealogy research process. If you need to get organized or learn something, the Roadmap still works, although you may need to get more creative with how you make a plan. This book only looks at research planning because it's more difficult. If you use the Roadmap for non-research, you can create a plan any way you like, just as you might plan a vacation or home project any way you like.

We'll go more in-depth with the research process later. Right now, the point is to understand that in addition to doing research, you need to plan what research you will do and "report" on what you found. Report was one of the five traditional steps, but it doesn't appear in the Brick Wall Solution Roadmap. That's because it is step three; "report" is covered by "write up your results."

This is perhaps the biggest change I made in explaining the research process. It is *not* a change in what an experienced genealogist would *do,* but it is very different from the traditional *explanation.* Because the Roadmap provides actionable steps, I didn't want it to be a list of dozens of steps, so I had to get creative.

With the Roadmap, you solve your problem at step three. Sometimes when you review your past research, you realize you found the solution; you just hadn't recognized it. You didn't solve the problem after doing research in that case; you solved it after a review.

You never solve the problem after doing research. You solve the problem when you consider everything together. This is more analysis, but instead of just breaking things down, you put those pieces back together differently to give you a solution. You always solve the problem when you consider everything together; if you don't, you risk your solution being wrong. Even if you find the date, place, or name you wanted when researching, the problem isn't solved unless you consider everything else you've done.

Here's a hypothetical example. A record could state a birthdate explicitly, 12 December 1932. You were trying to find that person's birthdate, so you think that's the answer. But what if you already have a date of marriage for that person, 6 June 1943? Do you think that person married at age ten?

Something is wrong. Your problem is *not* solved even though you found the birthdate. You found an answer, but it might be incorrect. Sure, the date of marriage could be incorrect, but you need to do more research before you call the problem solved. Considering everything together, after reviewing it (step two), allows you to solve a problem or recognize a problem isn't solved even though you found the exact piece of information you sought.

Repeating the Process

One of the problems I ran into while learning the traditional research process explanation was being led to believe I should perform the process once to solve a problem. Analyzing the problem—the traditional first step—was usually taught as the way you'd approach a new problem. This made it seem you should then plan your research and do research until you were ready to report on a solution. That is, you'd just keep researching until it was time to report. Here's how I understood the research process with this flawed understanding:

- Analyze your new problem
- Plan all the research you need to do to solve the problem
- Research
- Research
- Research
- [keep researching until you're done]
- Write a report explaining your conclusion

Genealogy rarely flows this simply, and continually researching is a huge cheat. Thinking the process is performed once, from start to solution, is one of the confusing issues with the traditional explanation. Even if your understanding is not as flawed as mine was, it can still be off.

Are you repeating planning and research multiple times while analyzing the problem and reporting just once? This is closer to how genealogy research should work but still not quite right. Beginners often think you do each action once for a problem. This makes both research planning and reporting a monumental task! Not surprisingly, planning and reporting are put off. Even conscientious genealogists will think they'll start or improve those skills later because they're too hard to do right now. Any of these variations on the genealogy research process are inaccurate, and if you're doing them, they are likely the reason you're repeatedly stuck.

A more accurate representation of the traditional research process explanation is:

- Analyze the current problem, taking into account whatever is new since the last analysis
- Plan research based on the preceding analysis

- Execute the research plan
- Analyze your findings
- Report on your findings
- Repeat

This can be viewed as a series of steps, but what to do still isn't clear to most genealogists. It is too easy to think you go through this process once for a problem.

No matter how it is explained, the genealogy research process is the process for doing one research session. That isn't one problem or one day. It is executing one plan or a part of a plan if you stop partway through. Sometimes you go through several plans in a day. Sometimes, it takes multiple days to complete a plan.

Before you start to sound like Jenni, lamenting the time this will take, realize that your review can simply be reading the summary you wrote at the end of your research day the previous day. It could be reading the summary you wrote an hour ago when you finished the previous research session. The point isn't to spend a set amount of time reviewing. The point is to ensure you are familiar with the relevant details and have considered everything, both your past work and your new findings.

When you were working on the same research problem minutes or an hour before, many details are fresh in your mind. The review prevents you from inadvertently missing something important. Writing down information and reviewing it is how you achieve this. You make it faster by summarizing at the end of each session so you don't have to review *everything*.

This should also make it obvious that Occasional Genealogists have it much harder than *often genealogists*. Having information fresh in your mind makes the full research process faster. The only way to overcome the issue of long breaks between research sessions is to take great notes. Your notes act like your memory but are so much more effective! It's fun to just hop around a research website finding new records, not taking notes or following a process. When you come back to that problem weeks, months, or years later, you'll probably have to hop around to the same records. It might be fun again, but it's certainly repetitive.

I'd never tell a genealogist they can't hop around a website clicking records and attaching "stuff" to their tree. Genealogy is a hobby, not a life-or-death situation. It should be fun. Do it how you want to do it. But recognize you might also be causing your own frustration because of your lack of process. Decide if you want to continue to grow your tree and if you want to build a correct tree, not just one populated with random names, dates, and places.

If you want to grow *your* tree, commit to slowing down and following the genealogy research process. The next chapter will teach you the shortcut to follow the process as fast as possible without cheating it.

***

Choose Your Process Explanation

I've given you two ways to look at the genealogy research process. Here they are side-by-side, so you can quickly refer to them and remember the version that resonates with you.

Traditional Explanation	Brick Wall Solution Roadmap
Analyze the problem	Step one, define the problem
	Step two, review existing research
	Step three, write up what you found
Plan research	Step four plan research
Research	Step five execute the plan
	(Step six repeat)
Analyze your findings	If needed, Step one, redefine the problem
	Step two, review existing research and new research findings together
Report on your findings	Step three, write up what you found
Repeat	(Continue to step four if your problem isn't solved)

Bring It All Together

A big takeaway from the comparison above should be that you need to review your past research more and take more notes. Not just notes while researching but recording your ideas and questions when you review, which is at the start and end of the traditional process. Bringing information together from multiple research and review sessions is what reporting is. You are telling yourself what you found when you looked at all your research together.

You should report to yourself whenever you need to tell your future self something. This can be an idea; *maybe that household enumerated next in the census is related.* It could be a question; *what does the term 'next friend' mean?* It could be an explanation of how you discovered the 1943 marriage date is wrong, and the 1932 birthdate is correct. If the term reporting sounds too hard and you shy away from it for that reason, think of a report as either notes or a summary.

This gets back to Jenni's conundrum. There will be so many notes from all that research. How do you have time to review it all?

That's the purpose of the traditional reporting step. Research notes are a summary of what happened at the moment you researched. You saw many documents and had many ideas. A report is a summary of your notes or several sets of notes. You should create a summary of your notes when you finish taking them. This makes it easy to review only the pertinent notes for your focused problem. You first read your summary to decide if that set of notes is pertinent to your current problem. If they are, you may need to read the notes. If they are not, you move on to read the next summary.

Once you start consistently planning your research, you will have many research sessions that you thought were important to complete, but often you only need to see the summary that you did not find what you were looking for in that source. This was one of the things traditionally kept in a research log, but that is easily tracked with digital notes today.

If you've been researching anything like Jenni, grabbing facts from sources, and that was all, the full process seems like a lot of extra work. As you research, it is a lot more work. But when you are stuck, having planned, reported, and researched gets you to a solution so much faster. Recognize this. Your individual research sessions will go slower when following the research process, but *you will find a solution faster.*

Every problem is unique, so it's not possible to gauge the time it takes to solve a problem while following the process versus not. But it is certain that some problems will never be solved if all you do is grab names, dates, and places. It's likely most of us have missed a solution because we came across it either when we had too little experience to recognize it as a solution or because we didn't have enough information to recognize it.

Example From the Author

Bud is a nickname for my ancestor Dennis. When I made that discovery, that's how I finally found my fourth great-grand-father's date of death. It had been in my notes almost since I had started researching that branch of the family tree twenty years earlier. I had notes, so I only wasted twenty years. Without notes, I don't know if I'd have figured out his date of death even today. The actual source I used is not online. The information is online, but it's not on a major website. It's not something I'd just stumble across during a random research session. If my past self had followed the research process correctly, reviewing new and old results routinely, I would have realized Bud was my great-grandfather much sooner. Who knows what other records about him I've overlooked!

Great genealogy requires a great research process. You don't need to invent a process; it has existed for years. You simply need to understand it and follow it.

Your Turn—Not Yet!

I've encouraged you to try several skills you've learned after each chapter, but this is a little different and critical point in this book. I don't recommend you try applying the research process quite yet.

Maybe you're feeling slightly nervous about a multi-step process you "need" to follow. Don't worry! Technology has made it much easier to follow the full process. Keep reading to learn the shortcut that makes great genealogy so much easier.

Chapter 5:
Essential Shortcut

"Imogene! Would you please stop coming up with more things I'm supposed to do for genealogy? This is hard enough without throwing in reviewing, planning, and reporting."

"I know, Jenni, but it's not really that hard. It sounds like a lot to do, but my cousin showed me a shortcut that rolls planning, note-taking, and reporting together. When doing it this way, you're just doing three things, not five. Defining your problem using the W-frame System, reviewing what you already know plus just learned, and taking notes."

"Am I taking notes or writing a report? Or creating a plan?"

Gene laughed, "Don't worry, it's almost all the same thing. We've already talked about taking notes. Almost all the information you were supposed to record in your notes should be in your plan and your report. Back when we used paper, they each had to be separate because, well, it was paper. A plan couldn't also be notes and a report. You can update a digital document so they can be one thing. It saves so much time versus creating three documents. Plus, it helps you stay focused on the problem you want to solve."

"That would be nice. Do you know last night, I spent four hours researching something totally different than what I sat down to do? And worst of all, I forgot to take notes, so I pretty much wasted four hours. I had to quit when I started to fall asleep, so I didn't find what I was looking for, and I don't remember what I did, either. I think I was making progress, but maybe it was all a dream."

"Yeah, I've had that happen. Something caught your eye, and you started chasing it down? It can be fun, but it's about as useful as a dream the next day."

"Exactly. I guess I do need this shortcut. That 'research' was fun, but I regret wasting those four hours now."

Learn the "Genealogy Roll-up" shortcut Gene's cousin taught her in the next section. It's my favorite shortcut, too.

***

The Genealogy Roll-up Shortcut

Previously, you learned what to include in your notes. Several of these items are the same as what you record in your research log. You've already learned the shortcut, where you can just use digital notes instead of keeping a research log. That's part of this Roll-up, but it gets even better.

> **Reminder:** If you take paper notes, you'll need to keep a separate tracking method. If the tracking method is paper-based, you need to keep a research log. Learn 20th-century techniques for tracking with paper. The Genealogy Roll-up only works if you take notes digitally.

When taking digital notes, you'll save the most time if you start your notes from your research plan. The information you need in your plan is generally the same as what you keep in your notes, minus your results. You then summarize what you found on page one of that document which is your "report." That's the entire shortcut!

You roll your plan into your notes and your notes into your report. You're creating one efficient roll-up that didn't cheat any of the research process. In fact, you're more likely to include all the necessary information when you use this shortcut.

> **By the way**: I didn't invent this concept, but I've tried to create a version (the Genealogy Roll-up) that gives you the most details to get you started. I want to point out that this isn't my original idea because you can learn more about it from many other sources, and I always recommend learning from a variety of sources. When I first learned to be a professional genealogist, I learned about "reporting as you go," which is a professional version of this technique.

> Once you've got the basics, that's a good phrase to learn more about. I've seen other educational material about turning your research plan into your research notes, although not a specific phrase associated with that half of the Genealogy Roll-up. Reading other people's explanations of how to roll these once distinct documents into each other can help you cement this concept in your mind. Think about the reason why we capture all this information, though, as sometimes people suggest cheats instead of shortcuts. The following chapters will help you

learn what information to include, and why, so you are equipped to judge a cheat from a shortcut for yourself.

You've learned how to take great research notes but not how to plan or report. The following chapters will cover planning and reporting in depth. Because this book is designed with Occasional Genealogists in mind, I'm going to give you the quick-start version in this chapter so you can get started using the Genealogy Roll-up as soon as you finish this chapter.

You'll get more out of the following chapters on pre-planning analysis, research planning, and reporting if you have tried this shortcut, so feel free to pause at the end of this chapter and apply this new skill. Just don't let yourself get bogged down if it seems hard. Give it a try, perhaps on a couple of different problems. Then come back and keep reading.

The Roll-up and Research Planning

In a later chapter, we'll go over how to create a research plan in-depth. It can take a while to get used to creating plans, so you might need to start using the Genealogy Roll-up before you've mastered research planning. I want to emphasize— *try* to create a plan.

Saving time using this Genealogy Roll-up makes it easier to add planning and reporting into your personal process. Not only does creating separate plans, notes, and reports take more time, but you would then also spend more time organizing three separate items. Although creating a plan, notes, and report is helpful versus skipping the process, reviewing them is what supercharges your research. That means you must be organized enough to find what you need to review.

Reality Check

Part of the point of *The Occasional Genealogist* blog is being realistic about doing hobby genealogy. When genealogy research is your job, you don't want to cheat the process. That's cheating your client. Lots of information about doing professional research is available. But it's hard to achieve that level as a hobbyist, especially when first learning skills like planning and reporting. So, I like to be realistic with genealogists still working on building their research process muscles.

Not planning your research is a cheat, but if you at least take great notes, that's better than planning research badly and taking bad notes. Great genealogy notes, as described in chapter three, can minimize the effect of cheating the research process. Use the note-taking template provided in the bonus material to guide you. Eventually, you'll remember to record this information without needing a template.

Takeaway: Better to take great notes and not plan than plan poorly and take poor or no notes.

Advantages of the Note-Taking Template

You'll learn research planning is probably much easier than you think, but it can be hard to break the habit of just researching without first planning. I came up with this specific template because it's a much easier first step to master instead of trying to learn planning, note-taking, reporting, analysis, research tracking, and everything else as fast as possible.

Great notes mimic as much of the full process as possible in one easy-to-learn skill. A template makes it easy by guiding you. Another way I like to refer to this is that the template is a tool, not a crutch. *You* wield a tool to achieve your goal. You *need* a crutch, whether you like it or not. Use genealogy templates, of any type, as tools. Don't rely on them like a crutch.

To take great notes, you have to pre-plan. Pre-planning happens in steps one through three of the Brick Wall Solution Roadmap, the steps before the planning step.

Pre-planning and taking great notes take you a long way toward the full genealogy research process. Just realize that skipping planning or reporting is a cheat. I'm not telling you it's right to skip planning and reporting. I'm telling you, if you do, great notes make it a much more minor cheat.

If you didn't already sign-up, get the bonus material at: https://genealogyskills.com/bonus/ .

Turn the Note-Taking Template into a Planning Template

One of the things I love about this note-taking template, and I've created quite a few over the years, is this one is easy to use as a planning template, too. I'll explain how to turn the note-taking template into a planning template.

Why don't I provide a planning template? I'm assuming you'll first use the note-taking template on sources you already used while you review. You want to review before you plan new research, and taking notes happens in a review. If you do this, not just try it but review and take lots of new notes, you'll likely identify some adjustments you want to make to the note-taking template. I'm saving you the time of also adjusting the planning template. You'll see the planning adjustments are very fast to make, although they take some explanation.

First Template Adjustment

First, select one very specific problem to solve. This is covered in a lot of detail in the following chapters. I recommend testing a hypothesis instead of asking a research question. The distinction between a hypothesis and a research question and why I recommend a hypothesis is explained later. For now, recognize your plan needs to be very specific. If you don't know how to pick a hypothesis to test, I have a simpler option you can start with.

To get started immediately, you want a plan that is easy to complete. This means focusing on one part of your

W-frame-defined problem. Until you fully understand how to create a hypothesis, the best way to do this is to pick a part of your *when* and *where* to focus on in one plan.

For example, maybe you're trying to identify a date and place of death. You have a record of the last time you know the person was alive. Let's say it was the 1880 U.S. federal census—*when* is 1880, and *where* is their residence. You don't have a way to determine when he was dead other than using something like "when he was 100"—or 120 if you want to really be safe!

Ideally, you only want to use between one and five sources in one plan. If you need more, that should be a different plan. One plan could focus on using up to five sources available for the state or county he last lived in. If twenty-five sources for the state were identified but only three for the county, create a plan to use the three for the county.

For one plan, you could also focus on using the only four sources you can think of for the state that covers 1890-1896. This is not defining your problem. You are picking a subset of your problem to research. Remember, we want a plan that is as easy to complete as possible and you will create multiple plans for one problem. If that means arbitrarily starting with easy and quick sources that cover a subset of your *when* or *where*, do it. Also, you don't need to smash five sources into a plan to maximize your plan.

You should have some kind of reasoning behind your selection of the one to five sources. For your first plans, you can use the following list to help you identify a reasonable group of one to five sources. This list can also be used as you get more experience, but you should also become better at planning and combining these considerations along with creating a hypothesis. Eventually, this will become second nature.

Considerations For Narrowing Your Problem to a Plan

Use one or more of these considerations to select between one and five sources for your plan. It is fine to use one of these options, which leads to only one source in one plan:

- Sources that are most likely to solve your problem.
- Sources that are fast and easy to use, including easy to understand.
- Sources for a subset of your *when*.
- Sources for a subset of your *where*.
- The only sources related to your project that you can access.
- Sources with information leading to more sources you can use.

Note: If your W-frame-defined problem leads you to only one obvious source to check or even less than six sources, you don't need to narrow down your problem for the plan. If that one source doesn't solve the problem, you will need to develop related problems to research or create relevant hypotheses to test.

Randomly picking a location or date range that yields less than six sources is not the best way to define one plan. It's effective when you don't have a better idea, though. I include an entire chapter on creating a hypothesis because it is a skill you may need to improve. Picking a good hypothesis is the best way to narrow your plan, but before your skills allow you to do that, use the considerations above so you can practice planning, even if your plans aren't great. You can make up for deficiencies in your plan with great notes.

As you're getting started with planning, keeping your plans to between one and five sources will help you easily create and complete your plans which gives you the practice you need. If you have a burning one, two, or up to five sources you want to use, create a plan. The whole idea is to start planning and keep it simple.

Second Template Adjustment

Second, record why solving that problem or using those specific sources is important to your main problem. This topic was mentioned as part of tracking and note-taking but per source. You should have a reason for creating the plan, whether it's the fact you can't think of any other sources to use for the problem or a very specific idea. Remember, you're recording this as part of your notes, not in a research log where you're limited to a little box you have to squeeze your handwriting into. Explain your reasoning for using these sources.

Here's what it might look like for the hypothetical example about the man last alive in the 1880 census, where you've decided to focus on the 1890 sources because you know of less than five of them.

> Research will begin with the four state-wide sources listing deaths for 1890–1896. This should cover a larger area in case he died outside the county [from the 1880 census]. However, there's no reason to think he died in this timeframe and not earlier or later. This is simply a quick and easy starting place.

Let's say, instead, your plan was for the only sources for the county if there were less than five. Your reason might look like this.

> This plan focuses on the only known sources which could list a death date and are available for [county, state] where he was last known to be alive in June 1880.

Explaining your reasoning or thought process goes back to the purpose of tracking all research. Whether you need to repeat using a source can depend on what was in your mind when you used it. That's why this needs to be recorded in your plan, even if it seems too obvious to bother with. Your why is a piece of information you cannot recapture later. You won't be sure of your exact reasoning at a later date. Make sure to include this as part of your plan, even if it seems obvious.

The above two examples would be for two different plans. If you're an Occasional Genealogist, you might only manage to create and execute one of these. There are consequences of skipping recording *why*. If you neglected to record your why for the state-wide sources, your future self might wonder if you had a good reason to believe he did not die in the county where he was living in 1880. If I wondered about that, I'd be scouring my notes for the evidence that led to that thought. But in this example, that evidence doesn't exist. Searching my notes for it would be a complete waste of time. Simply telling myself why I selected those sources saves me time in the future. I'd quickly move on to create the plan with the county sources if I knew I was simply planning based on the sources I was aware of.

For both planning and reporting, I've learned the hard way that I should treat my future self like a different person. She has the same ingrained knowledge as me. Whatever knowledge I know and don't forget, she knows it, too. So I don't need to include details like I would include for a client with an unknown knowledge level. But future me needs to have things explained as clearly as if you're explaining things to a different person. Both my husband and I have a terrible habit of starting a conversation in the middle of a thought we're having. My husband doesn't know what thoughts are inside my head and vice versa. I often have no idea who his pronouns refer to, and therefore, I have no clue what he is talking about. Make sure you add enough information so your future self understands what you're saying. It should not read like you're being dropped into the middle of someone else's thought.

Spend a few extra minutes to record *why* in your plan so your future self can follow your train of thought. I keep emphasizing *why* because it is so often left out. Your *why* for doing things, as well as other ideas you have while doing whatever work you are doing, are crucial. Understanding your thoughts at the time of research can speed up your future work, no matter if your ideas were good or not.

Third Template Adjustment

Third, have between one and five sources you plan to use to solve the problem. This is your actual plan. I'll explain later why I recommend between one and five sources per plan, but for now, use this guideline to get started. If you have more than five sources you want to use to solve a problem, record them as ideas in your notes—research note, review note, or random note so you don't forget the sources. Refine your problem for the one plan, so it only applies to between one and five sources.

The Obvious Template Adjustment

Finally, you won't have research results, so you are leaving this part of the note-taking template out of your plan. I mention this because past research results that seem important to include are background information, not research results. It's possible to cause confusion if you put background information under a heading for research results.

That's it. To use the note-taking template for planning, you simply add three items:

- The narrowed problem you are focusing on for this single plan.
- Why you selected that narrowed problem.
- Your planned sources, between one and five of them.

Comparing your plan to your *completed* notes, you're only adding one item, the narrowed problem. Your notes need to record each source you used, so you are entering those when you plan instead of when you research. You also have one reason for the plan instead of one reason for each source, so that's not a completely new item, either. If you can take great notes, you can easily create a research plan!

You can absolutely take great research notes. You've got a template to guide you. You might not be a note-taking ninja when you start, but you can do this. That means you can create a good research plan, if not a great one. Genealogy is a learnable skill which means you need to practice. So get started.

Reporting with the Genealogy Roll-up

When you finish your research session—either that plan, day, or source—report by adding a summary of your results to the start of your notes document. The purpose of this summary is to save you time when you review. You can just read the summary instead of all the notes. You only need to read the full notes if you decide that it is necessary for that specific situation.

This summary is ideally on page one, but you may have longer background information that bumps the summary off page one. The summary goes above your notes, but after any details you need to read while reviewing. For practical purposes, the only wrong place to put your summary is nowhere. Don't get hung up with where to write it; just get in the habit of reporting by summarizing your notes every time you finish them.

You should also write a summary when you review several sets of notes. That's step three of the Brick Wall Solution Roadmap. This is a separate action from writing a summary of the research notes you just created during your research in step five. You can think of a review summary as review notes, if you prefer, or call it a report to differentiate from your notes summary. It doesn't matter what you call it; just do it.

Recap:

- Create your research plan, ideally with a customized template.
- Take your notes directly on your (digital) plan.
- On page one of your plan/notes, write a summary of your findings.

If you've included the parts indicated in the provided note-taking template, this digital document becomes your plan, tracking method, notes, and report.

Section 2: Essentials for Great (Not Just Good) Genealogy

Chapter 6:
Essential Analysis

Jenni spent a few weeks reviewing her past research and taking notes on the records she had already found. This allowed her to practice taking notes and tracking research without being tempted to rush ahead with the excitement of finding new records. She wrote a few reports after reviewing several sets of her notes on one project. She was really getting the hang of this!

Jenni had been hesitant to try research planning, though. Her past research had kept her busy, but she started to have some ideas for new research. She gave research planning a try, but it wasn't as obvious as she hoped it would be. So, she called Gene to see if she'd teach her how to create a research plan.

When Gene arrived, she found Jenni's desk was no longer so clean. "Wow, Jenni, it looks like you're working a lot differently. I guess James doesn't tidy up your papers every night when he turns off the computer?"

Jenni laughed. "He probably would. But I make sure to finish up and clean up after myself so I know what I need to do the next time I can research."

"That's great. So what are all these papers?"

"Oh, these are related notes and reports I made. I find it easier to print what I need so I can look at it while I'm researching online. I find it easier to have the paper to refer to instead of switching between what I see on the monitor. But this part's going great. I've got a different problem I need your help with." Gene nodded for Jenni to go on.

"I'm struggling to create a research plan. I have some exciting ideas I've put in my notes, but I couldn't figure out how to create an actual plan. I tried, and after two hours, I just gave up."

"Wow, it shouldn't take two hours. I bet you're making this too hard. I know I did when I first started creating research plans. Research planning has two parts. I don't think we've talked about the analysis you need to do before you create the actual plan. You learned some of it when we discussed the W-frame System. But now we should talk about how to finish analyzing your problem so you can easily create a research plan. Once that analysis is done, creating the actual plan is fast and easy."

"Are you sure about this, Gene? I don't really want to get into analysis. I just want to research my family."

"Well, I'm sorry to tell you, you've already been doing analysis. Research always involves analysis. Otherwise, you're just collecting pieces of information, and not necessarily the pieces of information you want. But don't worry, it sounds complicated, but it's not. If you like researching your family history, you like doing analysis; you just need to understand what analysis is and how to do it better!"

In the next section, learn what analysis is and how to do the most basic analysis before creating a research plan.

***

Analysis can be boiled down to something simple—asking questions. It's important to realize that although we often talk about "analyzing the problem" as the start of the research process, and sometimes you'll see "analysis and correlation" as part of the research step or as a step after it, you should do analysis continuously during the entire genealogical research process. There's never a wrong time to do analysis because there's never a bad time to ask a question.

This chapter is about genealogical analysis and the basic questions you should ask *before* you create a research plan. We'll start with understanding how the word analysis is used in genealogy. If you get confused and second-guess yourself because you don't understand how the term analysis is used for genealogy, you'll still have a significant problem even after learning the basic questions to ask.

What is Analysis

As you learned with the W-frame System, analysis is breaking something down. A chemical analysis identifies the chemicals or elements that make up whatever is being tested. A market analysis identifies opportunities or weaknesses in a market, defined for whatever decision a business is trying to make. But these are also equivalent to answering questions. "What is this substance made of?" "How many people pass this corner at rush hour; what's their average income; do they like coffee?" Each of these types of analyses is done differently.

Genealogical analysis is essentially answering questions. We analyze by finding answers to the questions *or* by performing other actions. Those other actions are also referred to as analysis. The double use of analysis can be confusing to newer genealogists. Is analysis something specific you do? Is it one action? Can you choose how to do it? Is it a nebulous concept—not something you do, but something you think about?

Analysis is *not* one thing. It can be a choice of actions or a concept. If you are told, "You need to do analysis," you are told to pick an action to analyze the problem. If we say, "Genealogy requires analysis," it's similar to saying, "You have to think about the problem."

To further confuse the novice, genealogists use the word analysis as both a noun and a verb. First, you analyze the information. Your analysis—the verb—is not complete until you write up an analysis—the noun—explaining the thought process you went through. For hobbyist genealogists, you do not need to create a formal written analysis. Simply explain the results of your analysis in sentences and paragraphs. I'll provide some additional information about writing an analysis at the end of the chapter on reporting.

Now that you've learned the indistinct ways genealogists toss around the word analysis, let's look specifically at analyzing the problem so you can create a research plan.

Basic Problem Analysis for Research Planning

You've already learned the W-frame System, a series of questions to break your problem down into the core elements needed (who, what, when, and where). Following the W-frame System is simple analysis. You need the W-frame answers to create a research plan. Ask one more question to complete the most basic analysis needed.

The basic question you need to ask next is, "How can I solve this problem?" I'll add this as *how*. If you think of ten specific sources you can use, you're ready to create a research plan. The analysis is done; you asked and answered *how* in a way that allows you to create a plan.

If you stare blankly into space when asking yourself *how* you either have to do more analysis or learn about how to solve the problem. If you recall, the Brick Wall Solution Roadmap is designed to help you learn how to solve a problem; step four will be creating an education plan. An education plan is simply an actionable plan to gain knowledge. If that is your situation, figure out how to learn the information—make a plan, execute that plan, and repeat back to the start of the Roadmap. You'll then end up back at asking yourself *how*.

The Process with Planning

When you ask yourself *how* you'll naturally want to consider your previous research and any information you have about related source types. In other words, you want to *review* your past research and source knowledge before arriving at ideas for the *best* sources to use for your plan. You define your problem in step one of the Roadmap, and if you're going to create a research plan, you should automatically want to review, that is, step two of the Roadmap.

Without the review, you might have ideas for ten sources, but perhaps you already used all ten of them. You *can* use them again, but that probably is not the best idea unless you have a good reason. You have to review your previous work and information to determine the best next step.

This simplified analysis, the W-frame System plus *how*, should naturally work hand-in-hand with steps one through three of the Roadmap if you want to create a research plan.

Research planning can seem daunting, and trying it can be hard. This sense of overwhelm is often due to thinking the genealogy research process is followed once to solve a problem. This train of thought suggests you would need to create one massive plan. However, now that you know you'll go through the whole process for a single research session and create a plan with no more than five sources, you'll realize plans are not that big.

In the next chapter, we'll explore creating a research plan. At this point, you should understand what analysis is in genealogy. It's not one thing. You should also know the five questions that make up the most basic analysis for creating a research plan: the four Ws plus *how*.

The other key point at this stage is understanding that you might start the Roadmap and need to create an education plan instead of a research plan. Research planning isn't easy until you answer, "How can I solve this problem?" To answer that question, many options are often available. You can't create a research plan if you can't come up with any answer to *how*, though.

Recap:

- You must define the W-frame elements as the most basic analysis for any research plan (who, what, when, and where).
- You need to review your past research to avoid repeating work inappropriately. Your review can also reveal clues you missed.
- You need a written result from your basic analysis and review.
- If you can't answer "How can I solve this problem," you need to focus on education. Create an education plan instead of a research plan.

Bonus: Different Ways to Learn "How to Solve This Problem?"

Depending on your genealogical experience, you may think the only way to answer "How can I solve this problem" is to learn about a source that will directly answer whatever problem you are trying to solve. In other words, if your question is "Who is John's father," you will try to learn about sources that will state who John's father is. If your problem is finding the burial location of an ancestor, you might think you need to learn what websites list all the burials for a certain location. You might try to learn a variety of things, though.

Learning about specific sources that can provide the exact information you want is one approach to answering, "How can I solve this problem?" Another option is learning about *alternative information* that can provide your desired answer or offer additional clues to lead you to your desired answer. You'd then learn what sources provide that alternative information.

Similar, but different, is learning what alternative problems you should try to solve to provide clues to your main problem. We'll touch on this option a bit more in the next chapter when discussing selecting a hypothesis to test for your research problem. You may not need to learn about sources at all in this case. You might already have the needed source knowledge.

Another learning path is learning to use sources differently or recognizing clues in sources. Once again, you may not need to learn about new sources. These last two options, researching an alternative problem or getting more clues from known sources, can be great if limited sources are available for the time and place of your problem. They are also great options if the sources aren't so limited, but your access to them is.

For example, you might be limited by needing to research online, in a specific physical location, or when you need to stick to a research budget. Really tenacious genealogists have often discovered other sources that exist—but that doesn't mean they can access those sources. In such cases, you can either set the problem aside or learn other ways to solve the problem using the sources you can access.

A later chapter covers learning about sources. The above are educational options for answering "How can I solve this problem" unrelated to learning about sources. All genealogists need to know how to do both.

Bonus Recap:

- Learn about sources that could provide the answer you are seeking.
- Learn about alternative information you can use to answer your question or that can lead to an answer.
- Learn about alternative problems you can solve that will provide clues to your main problem.
- Learn to use known sources differently. This can be by better understanding what the source is telling you or learning what clues it provides and how to use those clues.

Chapter 7:
How to Create a Research Plan

"**G**ene, is it time to start learning to create a research plan yet?"

"Yes, Jenni, you've got all the elements to learn how to create a great research plan."

Feeling impatient to get planning like Jenni? In the next section, learn how easy it is to create a research plan since you've already learned how to analyze your problem and take notes.

***

Just as analyzing the problem came through answering five simple questions, planning research is far simpler than you probably think. If you don't first analyze the problem, research planning is almost impossible.

Let's review what you should have before you start creating a research plan. You defined the problem following the guidelines in the W-frame System.

The W-frame System (Review)

Who is the subject of my problem—one person, couple, or family as is appropriate for your *what*?

What one event or relationship is my problem about?

When does the event or relationship take place?

Where does the event occur, or where does the person live during the *when*?

Reminder: If you don't have all four "W" elements, you are not ready to work on that problem. You need to back up to do additional research to find the missing element or elements. If your problem is finding a when or where you still need some type of constraint for that element. This could be a timeframe instead of an exact date or a limited number of options for *where* for the event.

You may need to reframe your problem to have all of the elements. For example, your *who* isn't the unknown father you are seeking. You don't have sufficient *when* and *where* constraints for him. Instead, it is the child whose father you are seeking. This person you have researched so you can meet the W-frame System requirement. It is acceptable, and sometimes necessary, to reframe the same problem several times and approach it differently. You'll get even better at this as you learn to plan research.

Once you have the four required elements for a genealogical problem, ask yourself, "How can I solve this problem?" Once you've answered that question, you create a plan.

OK, maybe that still seems like a big task.

Research plans are *not* big. That is where most genealogists go wrong and why Jenni was spending two hours working on a plan *after* the analysis was done.

There are three basic sections to a genealogy research plan:

1. Analyzed problem
2. Background information
3. The plan—a short list of exact sources to check

Those first two sections are created in pre-planning, meaning they should be done before you are ready to create the plan. It can take many hours to complete pre-planning. It can also take minutes. It all depends on where you're starting from.

You need one additional item that isn't an entire section. It was referenced in the chapter on the Genealogy Roll-up. This item is a hypothesis. You can put the hypothesis anywhere in your plan, at the top, after the background information, whatever you prefer. You just want to have it. You can't create the actual plan without it, and it is based on the analyzed problem and the background information. Hence the flexibility of its placement.

> **Hint**: A plan's layout, format, or order is not what makes it a plan. There is an order to the information that makes more sense so you can use the plan, including reviewing your rolled-up plan, more efficiently. Do not let the layout trip you up. You may need to create plans and use the Genealogy Roll-up for a little while before discovering the best flow for you. Research planning templates are a tool for beginners

to get started faster. They are not a requirement. Creating a *customized* template for yourself helps even the most experienced genealogist work as fast as is reasonable.

Your plan should test one hypothesis instead of planning all possible research. We'll take a detailed look at this in the next chapter. As with learning the Genealogy Roll-up, you can start using this information now, so I've saved the additional details for later.

As you cement research planning into your brain, you want to remember you need one hypothesis to test, and the plan only has three simple sections. If you prefer to think of this as a series of questions, remember this:

- What problem am I trying to solve? (your analyzed W-frame problem)
- What one hypothesis will *this* plan test?
- What background information is relevant to this hypothesis?
- What sources will I use to test my hypothesis?

Creating an *Actionable* Plan

A research plan is a list of specific sources you will look at. If you answered "How can I solve this problem" by thinking of *types* of sources, that could lead to dozens and dozens of specific sources. That isn't an *actionable* plan. If you have too many ideas to know where to start, that's not actionable.

If you have so many specific sources in your plan you can't finish it, that isn't actionable either. You did take the action of doing research, but you didn't take action on some sources, and you missed the action steps that happen when you finish a plan. Although we might not use all the sources in our plan, we want to finish the plan.

An actionable plan is a plan you finish. Finishing a plan happens when you use all the sources or actively decide you are finished even though all the sources weren't used. A plan is not called finished if you were interrupted and forgot about it. A plan is not finished if you give up because it's too hard.

> **Important!** You create one plan for a problem at a time. We'll talk about why later, but if you don't finish a plan, you technically should not create another plan for that problem. This might be a good mental trick to remind yourself an actionable plan is one you complete. Without completing it, you aren't allowed to continue working on that problem!

Testing a hypothesis leads to actionable, and therefore completable, plans. Research planning is almost like making genealogy a series of toddler tasks. You don't give a toddler a list of things to do, and certainly not with a flowchart where they have to decide which option to pursue based on an outcome of a previous task. That's way too complicated for a toddler, even if they are bright enough to help with the laundry or put away the clean dishes.

Genealogy *is* complicated. What you do next does depend on what just happened. But that isn't part of a research plan. That is analysis. A research plan tells you what research you will do next. That's it. It is just a plan. It isn't the research; it isn't the analysis. *It is not a flowchart.*

I have created a flowchart to explain the research process before. It's hard. There are many options in genealogy. Just remember your research plan should never involve a flowchart. The only "option" in your research plan is deciding to actively end the plan before all the sources are used.

A flowchart is something larger than a plan. A flowchart is analysis. Analysis happens throughout the research process except while planning. Research planning is toddler-simple. You can think of it like a mental break in the process. You've done the hard part; now, just put the pieces together. If research planning seems more difficult than making a simple list of tasks, you aren't done with your analysis, or you need education or organization. You'll see how this works in a moment.

The next chapter will talk about creating a hypothesis. First, let me summarize how you include your analyzed problem and background information. Your plan does not need fancy formatting. If you like a nice-looking plan, do it. If you like simplicity, do it. The information is needed to keep you focused, and so you know where you started. If you are using the Genealogy Roll-up, you want the information from the first two sections available when you review your summary and notes, which are created from the plan.

Analyzed Problem

Your analyzed problem is the statement you created from the W-frame System. If you didn't use the W-frame System, it at least needs the W elements. We will select one hypothesis to test for this plan, but we need to know the main problem we are trying to solve. That means we include our W-framed problem or an equivalent statement with the W elements.

This is as easy as it sounds, adding a statement. When creating your plan, copy and paste this from the written W-frame definition you previously created. Planning is step four, and all the previous steps should be *complete* before you start step four. Creating this statement is step one of the Roadmap and needs to be done before step two, which is done before step three. You don't have to come up with the analyzed problem while planning; it is already done.

Background Information

The background information includes whatever background you believe is vital for this particular plan. It might be copied and pasted from a previous summary or report. You might be compiling bits of knowledge from different notes. This decision is yours.

If you haven't gathered background information, including sources, you didn't use that information to reach the planning phase. Background information collected after step three technically is not background information for this plan, even if it is related. *Gathering* background information is part of step two. Remember, the Roadmap is a series of steps you complete in order. If you start step four, planning, and then decide to bring in more background information, you should back up and review that information and write a new summary (step three). Sometimes you do want to stop planning to do a further review or pre-planning analysis. The point is not that this is wrong. The point is research planning is simple once pre-planning is done.

Simplifying Background Information in a Plan

Background information is crucial, but don't stall over it. The best way to simplify it is to only include what is necessary. If you feel it is important to bring together a lot of information from different notes or summaries, what you are trying to do is write a report. Reporting is step three of the Roadmap. Finish it before step four, planning.

Another way to keep background information simple is to recognize it is perfectly acceptable if your background information is the same for multiple plans. When you think about this background information, which is analysis, you might devise different ways to answer, "How can I solve this problem?" These could be different plans because they answer the question differently but are all based on the same background information.

Understanding the Roll of Background in Your Plan

Just imagine the difference if you are trying to find a father. For one plan, you had the child's birth year as 1855. For another, you had a birth date of 1845. This would change the first sources you considered, but if the problem continued to be unsolved, it would also affect your options going forward.

If the child was born in 1845, the father could be long-dead by 1855. Your research would shift purely by this one piece of information being different.

I have this actual problem in my family tree. I can't confirm if a man was born in the 1850s or ten years earlier. I'm slowly working through research options until the problem is solved. It makes a difference knowing how I'm dealing with the man's birth year or age for each research phase.

Now that you're convinced you need to include background information, we'll cover the basics of creating a hypothesis for your plan so you can practice before learning more in-depth information about picking a good or great hypothesis for your plan.

What Is a Hypothesis?

A hypothesis is something you will test. You may be familiar with this from school science classes where you had to hypothesize what would happen when you combined chemicals. Your hypothesis might be, "The liquid will turn purple when we combine x and y." For a research plan, a hypothesis is also a *statement*. You will test if the statement is true or false without worrying about blowing up the chemistry lab. It will *sound* like a statement of fact, but we haven't tested whether it *is* a fact, yet.

Sometimes genealogists are told their research plan needs a research question to answer. This is a different approach to research planning. I prefer the hypothesis so much that I don't even list a research question as an option. Just realize that you may hear that your research plan needs a research question to answer. Instead, I always teach that your plan needs a hypothesis to test. The next chapter will go more in-depth on question versus hypothesis, as it can be tricky to create a narrow plan without this understanding. For now, we'll stick with the basics.

Our example problem from Jenni is "Who is Henry Alford's father?" She defined her problem with the W-frame System in this way:

> Who is the father of Henry Alford, born 10 December 1850 in Alabama and died 11 May 1913 in Geneva County, Alabama.

Jenni's main *question* is, "Who is Henry's father?" That's a big question to try to answer. You could create multiple hypotheses for that one question. Here are some examples of types of hypotheses for this question:

- Robert is Henry's father.
- Samuel is Henry's father
- Henry's father died about two years before Martha had Henry's oldest known (possible) half-sister. Henry is listed as the heir of his father in probate records.
- Henry is listed as the son of his father in *XYZ* will book.

One of the great things about using a hypothesis is you can test conflicting answers, such as the first two examples. The last example shows how you can turn an idea for a specific source to check—wills—into a hypothesis. The third example is creating a hypothesis that is truly a hypothesis, something you think might be true and want to test. We'll examine these again in more detail in the following chapter about hypotheses.

Next Steps:

You now know what a hypothesis is, so you can add that element to research planning with the Roll-up. If you're excited to start research planning, do it. You can try it out before reading the next chapter. If, instead, you're ready to learn more about creating more advanced research plans, continue to the next chapter.

Examples from Jenni and Gene

Here are examples from two of Jenni's projects.

> **Problem:**
> Determine if Franklin Timothy Jones (born 1894 in MS), husband of Elizabeth Greeson, is the same as Frank T. Jones, that died in New York City on 22 December 1932. Family members say these are the same man. Franklin abandoned Liza and disappeared before the 1930 census.
> **Possible Hypotheses:**
> - Frank Jones has a death certificate listing he was born about 1894 in Mississippi.
> - Frank Jones has an obituary from a New York newspaper listing his children, including those he had with Liza.

This particular problem would quickly require more than a simple hypothesis if the above ideas for specific records could not be found or obtained or if they were inconclusive on the point of whether Franklin and Frank were the same man. We'll look at an alternative approach in an example in the next chapter.

Problem:

Who is the father of Albert David Hockë, born in Kentucky in 1858, died in Arizona in 1907. He married and lived in Cincinnati until moving out west around 1900. He hasn't been found in census records prior to 1900. The spelling of his surname is unclear, though.

Hypothesis:

Albert left a death certificate in Arizona or obituary in Arizona or Cincinnati.

The next chapter will talk about picking a hypothesis that leads to a plan you can complete. That could be an issue with the hypothesis above. Given that only a year of death is known, too many records need to be searched. Here's another hypothesis that is an option for this problem.

Alternative Hypothesis:

Albert was christened in 1858 or 1859 in a German Lutheran church in Cincinnati or adjoining areas in Kentucky.

You would create this hypothesis because you would need to check less than six sources. This hypothesis is very specific. The timeframe is two years, and this is only for German

Lutheran churches (a denomination). This hypothesis doesn't include other types of Lutheran churches, even if they have a predominately German membership. Jenni's pre-planning analysis would lead her to this hypothesis. You aren't seeing all of that analysis, but it is necessary to reach this hypothesis.

***

Here are examples from other projects besides Jenni's. Once again, you don't see the pre-planning analysis; you should assume it is complete. These examples show how a hypothesis is narrower than the original problem.

> **Problem:**
> Who are the parents of Raffaele "Ralph" Desiderio (b. abt 1870 Salerno, Italy–d. 9 Apr 1952 Branford, CT). Raffaele immigrated to Branford from Scafati, Salerno, Italy in 1912.
> **Hypothesis:**
> Raffaele was christened in a Catholic church in Scafati between 1869 and 1872.

> **Problem:**
> Who is "Gaetano Giordano" father of Michela (Giordano) Desiderio (abt. 1873, Italy–Dec. 1949 New Haven Co., CT). Michela came to Branford, CT, with her husband and children from Scafati, Italy. Her father was listed as Gaetano Giordano, a resident of Scafati.

Hypothesis:

Only one Gaetano Giordano can be found in city directories, living near Raffaele Desiderio in Scafati between 1900 and 1912.

Problem:

When did Berry S. Rigdon (c. 1787 SC to c. 1876 Irwin Co., GA) marry Mary Taylor (c. 1805 GA–before 1870)? They likely married between when the 1830 and 1840 U.S. federal census was enumerated. Mary could have had a previous marriage as Berry supposedly did (this means the name of the bride might not be "Taylor"). The marriage likely took place in the area around Appling County, Georgia, as Mary was a native of the area, and Berry lived there as early as 1830.

Hypothesis:

A Mr. Rigdon married a Mary or Polly in Appling County, Georgia, between 1830 and 1840.

Chapter 8:
All About Hypotheses

Gene and Jenni met a few weeks later to continue working on research planning. Jenni had been impatient to keep going, but Gene had a family vacation scheduled. Once Jenni dragged all the details of the trip, and a few pictures, out of Gene, Gene finally got Jenni back onto the topic of genealogy.

"So, Jenni, you've had weeks to focus on your research. Tell me how your research planning is going."

"Um..."

Gene was more than a little surprised by this response. Jenni had been excited to keep working, but Gene had a lot to do before the vacation, so they hadn't been able to meet. Gene had assumed Jenni was ready to work on her own. Had she missed explaining something?

"Jenni," Gene paused before ferreting out the deficiency in her teaching, "was there something you didn't know how to do? I thought you would just keep rolling along." That was clever, Gene thought, *rolling* along, referencing the Genealogy Roll-up. Jenni apparently hadn't caught the unintentional pun. Gene's smile faded as she asked, "What was the problem, Jenni? Was there something I forgot to explain?"

"Oh, no! It's not that. I think I've got it. It's just, well, I was so impatient to keep going. But I got a little sidetracked. I'm embarrassed I was so pushy about meeting again and then didn't even do any genealogy until last night. You see, I had the bedroom painted. And then I needed to get new linens for the bed, and then the bathroom didn't match, so..." Jenni realized all the details of why she hadn't done any genealogy didn't matter and just trailed off.

Gene laughed. "That's great! So how'd it go picking back up last night?"

Jenni finally smiled. "Actually, it *was* great. It took me about fifteen minutes to read the relevant notes on the project I was working on, and I was ready to get going like that master suite revamp never happened. I can't believe how I've been torturing myself for not following a process until now! I would never have gotten caught up so fast. The only problem was I stayed up way too late doing some new research on my Alford project. I made good progress; I'm just tired."

Jenni had a thoughtful look on her face as she paused. "I'm wondering if I should set the Alford problem aside for a while. I'm sure there's more online research I can do, but I feel like it might be better to wait and make a research trip to Alabama so I have access to more complete records instead of a little of this and a little of that, which is online."

"That's definitely an option, Jenni. Sometimes it is better to set a project aside. Every genealogist has plenty of projects to choose from. Even if you can do online research on one, it might not be as good a use of your time versus doing online research on a different project and waiting to do offline research on the first project.

"But let's look at your Alford project and some more advanced research planning. I only just got you started creating research plans before my vacation. I know you're focused on this Alford project. You might need to do some important online research before making a research trip. Great research planning ensures you've done all the preliminary research needed."

"OK. Here's my W-frame-defined problem." Jenni pointed to a piece of paper with the following problem typed out.

> Who is the father of Henry Alford, born 10 December 1850 in Alabama and died 11 May 1913 in Geneva County, Alabama.

"I asked myself how I could solve this problem. I made this list of ideas." Jenni handed Gene a handwritten list.

> Henry Alford's death certificate
> ~~Henry's birth certificate~~
> Henry's baptism or christening record
> Wills for Alford men in ??? County, Alabama between ???
> ~~Tax records for _____ County, Alabama about ___? (when Henry was 18-21)~~
> Marriage for a Martha and an Alford man in ??? County, Alabama, or nearby areas or along possible migration route.
> Deeds showing Henry got land from his father.

"These are good ideas, Jenni. Why did you cross some of them out?"

"Well, I learned birth certificates weren't kept in Alabama when Henry would have been born. For the tax records, I saw a suggestion that you might find a young man listed in his father's house because he was legally required to be taxed, which is usually at either age 18 or 21, depending on the law. But I don't think Henry's father was alive when Henry got to be that age. I think he was long dead, so even if the birth date I have is off by a few years, the tax records wouldn't lead to finding his father."

"That's good reasoning. But what if you learn something later that changes that assumption?" Jenni could tell Gene was testing her. She thought for a moment. "I guess I should keep these ideas in my notes. Then I can always use them if something changes."

"Yes!" Gene was pretty excited Jenni was getting this. Maybe she hadn't explained things badly. "I have another suggestion, though. You should also make notes of what you just explained to me. You only just learned about using the tax records to prove, or hint at, a father. When you need this suggestion later, you might not remember what you learned. You don't have to put things in your personal notes that you will definitely remember, but if you just learned something, write it down.

"Noting why you're not using a source can sometimes make a difference in the future. It might make it faster to skip over that idea again or make you realize you should reconsider it. All kinds of notes are so important in genealogy. Today is not tomorrow or next year. What's in your mind will change, your research will eventually change, and accessible sources will change."

"You're right, Gene. I only remembered why they were crossed off after I thought about it when I reviewed my notes last night. I remembered about the births not being recorded, but I had to think about what my tax list note meant!"

"I get it. If only we had perfect memory, genealogy would be so much easier." Both women laughed at this impossibility.

Gene took another look at the list before getting back to helping Jenni. "So why do you think you should make a research trip? I know what I'd do, but I'd like to hear what you're thinking."

"Honestly, I'm not sure what research plan to create first. I'm missing a lot of information. For example, I don't know what church would have a baptism record for Henry. I don't even know what religion he was.

"I don't know where his father died—if he did die early and not just run off. So I don't know where to look for a will. I could create a research plan to start with the first county I find Henry in, but I know I might end up needing to search all of Alabama. If he didn't leave a will, how would I know when to stop looking?

"I've got a similar problem with Martha remarrying. First, I'm assuming he's Henry's mother. I think I can use that assumption for now, though. But I'd want to search all Alabama marriages. I thought I could do that online, but when I started looking closely at the results I was getting, I realized there were counties I was missing results from, likely counties she married in, too. It seems like it'll be a lot of work to be sure I've fully researched that option because I know so little.

"Last night, I was all ready to try the deed option. Then I discovered deeds often aren't searchable. I might be able to do that research online, reading the microfilmed deeds that have been digitized. But I think there are a few counties where the deeds aren't online. It's a lot of work, I'm not sure Henry even owned land, and I would still need to access some deeds offline to be sure I checked every reasonable location."

Jenni let out a quick breath in frustration and turned to Gene, who inexplicably had a Cheshire cat grin on her face, "What are you smiling about?!"

"I'm so proud of you, Jenni. A few weeks ago, you were just hopping around the internet, taking whatever information came in front of you and nothing more. Now you're thinking about other options. Better yet, you're thinking about your best options."

"I guess so," Jenni said a little reluctantly.

"Don't worry; you're on the right track. We didn't get into how to create and pick a *good* hypothesis for your research plan. That's a tricky skill, but it can change your research. It'll help you deal with all these issues you're facing on this Alford problem."

Learn more about creating and using a good hypothesis in a research plan in the following section.

***

Going from Question to Hypothesis

Testing a hypothesis is what keeps plans small and actionable. Having a question doesn't automatically lead to actionable plans. By testing a hypothesis, you're forced to create a narrow plan versus if you ask a question. Jenni's list of ideas included a lot of overwhelming research options. Good research planning addresses or even avoids such options.

To fully help you understand, we'll first look at a question versus a hypothesis.

A Research Question

Jenni was trying to plan for a question she had. Her question was, *who was Henry's father*?

Jenni's list includes good ideas for how to find a father. As she clearly understands, this isn't an actionable plan. That's why Jenni got stuck. To create a plan you can follow, you'd need to identify exact sources to obtain. Baptisms, wills, marriage records, and deeds are all *types* of sources.

Jenni recognized she needed to know Henry's religion to identify specific baptism records. A location and time frame was needed to identify specific wills, marriage records, and deeds. This should sound an awful lot like the W-frame elements! The death certificate type of source can be turned into one specific source since Jenni knows where and when Henry died. The other ideas are too open-ended.

If Jenni wanted to create an actionable plan for all these ideas that listed the exact sources to check, it would likely take weeks of additional work. It would potentially still not be actionable because of the final plan's size.

Weeks of additional research to identify exact sources for all these ideas is a task that *can* be done, but it's not necessary. A smaller plan is a better idea. Jenni's concerns had her on the right track to a smaller plan, but she didn't quite know how to get there. Jenni has at least two options, creating a better hypothesis or picking a sub-problem.

Hypothesis Versus Sub-problem

One way to create a smaller plan is to break your problem down or answer a related problem. Sometimes that is your best option, but Jenni doesn't need to do that yet. A better option is to test a hypothesis. One hypothesis per plan. I'll give you examples of how this works in a moment, but first, you should understand how testing a hypothesis for a plan and breaking a problem down in pre-planning are similar but different.

This division of such similar ideas is a large part of why the genealogy research process is so powerful when you correctly understand it. First is the pre-planning phase, which is almost all analysis. You can also think of this as the *consideration phase* because you are considering or thinking about the problem. You can use whichever word best resonates with you, pre-planning or consideration.

During her consideration phase, Jenni learned about using tax records to prove or hint at a father-son relationship. She also further analyzed her specific problem and decided tax records were unlikely to work in her particular situation. That was analysis and consideration before getting to actual planning.

Next is the action phase, which starts with creating a plan and finishes with research. I like thinking of a consideration phase as a contrast to the action phase. You need action and thought in genealogy. You can't take action without first thinking about your problem in-depth. Jennie's consideration phase resulted in that entire list, not just the idea of using tax records.

Identifying a related sub-problem is also part of analysis. It happens in the consideration phase. Identifying a related sub-problem happens as step one of the Roadmap when you've looped back and need to refine your problem because it clearly hasn't been solved.

A hypothesis is based on the problem or sub-problem from step one of the Roadmap. Remember, the hypothesis is a *statement* you can test as true or false. Sometimes this is a sub-problem turned into a statement, but usually, it is one of several hypotheses that can be created. In other words, often, a hypothesis is even more specific than a sub-problem.

Sub-problem Example

We'll look at a simple sub-problem example from one of Jenni's other projects. You saw this problem in the previous chapter's examples, where several simple hypotheses were presented. Those were so simple we'll assume easy plans were completed for them.

> **Main Problem:**
>
> Determine if Franklin Timothy Jones (born 1894 in MS), husband of Elizabeth Greeson, is the same as Frank T. Jones, that died in New York City on 22 December 1932. Family members say these are the same man. Franklin abandoned Liza and disappeared before the 1930 census.
>
> **Hypotheses for two completed plans:**
>
> - Frank Jones has a death certificate listing he was born about 1894 in Mississippi.
> - Frank Jones has an obituary from a New York newspaper listing his children, including those he had with Liza.

Let's say we've had no luck with the death certificate or obituary helping us determine whether these men are the same or different. Either Frank's death certificate wasn't found, or it didn't list him born about 1894 in Mississippi. That hypothesis was false. The other hypothesis was also false due to an obituary not being found or Liza's children weren't listed as his children in it.

Since those simple options didn't work, this problem might best be solved by identifying a sub-problem.

Recognize that focused research would have been completed to first get the death certificate and then an obituary. These plans were so specific the negative hypotheses indicate the next best step is not trying to get the death certificate or an obituary. That was the only objective of each plan.

This is very different than sticking the name, dates, and places in a generic online search form and not finding what you wanted. In the case of the death certificate, once that plan is complete, if the death certificate was not found, it won't be found by trying again. Jenni had a specific date and place for the death certificate. If she didn't get it, either it was inaccessible, destroyed, or her information was wrong. She needs to try something else. The purpose of the Roadmap is to stop performing the same action repeatedly, hoping you'll get a different result. Jenni tried something specific. It didn't work. Now she can try something else specific.

Selecting a sub-problem further focuses research. A plan focuses on getting specific sources. A sub-problem allows the researcher to gather more information before deciding on another hypothesis to test.

> **Sub-problem:**
> Find Frank T. Jones's earliest residence in New York City.

This is not a hypothesis. Here's how we'd turn this into a hypothesis.

> **Hypothesis:**
> Frank Jones appears in New York City directories, indicating he lived there since well before the 1930 census.

You might create a sub-problem because it has few hypotheses to test. In other words, you select a sub-problem because you can work through its research quicker than the research for a different problem. In the Jones example above, if we could determine Frank lived in New York City while Franklin was living with Liza, that indicates they are separate men.

However, the sub-problem might also result in being unable to find Frank in early enough records to say they are different men. The information learned still affects future research. Other sub-problems won't focus on New York City records before when Frank was found in New York City. The sub-problem can shape what we do next, even if it doesn't solve the main problem.

Why This Hypothesis Creates an Actionable Plan

You've been instructed to create easy-to-finish plans with between one and five sources. If you aren't familiar with researching New York City directories, the Jones hypothesis example may not seem like a good choice for an actionable plan. Hopefully, you understand why the sub-problem was a good idea; the results can shape future research in many ways, whether the associated hypothesis is true or false. You need to understand the background of a problem to see why some hypotheses lead to an actionable plan.

This example assumes no city directories have been used. The previous research that led to the new sub-problem involved death certificates and obituaries. At this point, the plan for this hypothesis would be a one or two source plan—I'm using my knowledge of using New York City directories as part of my analysis; I'm not a New York or even urban research expert. Your plans will always be based on your own experience, so my lack of expertise is not a problem. This is how every genealogist must work. My analysis leads me to believe this hypothesis can be tested with one source.

I could also create an education plan to determine if my initial plan should only use one source or two. This education plan is so simple I wouldn't create a separate education plan but make notes in my report. This education plan is checking what years are included in the online searchable city directories I'm aware of. Once again, this is based on my knowledge and experience. Your education plan would be based on your knowledge and experience.

I created this hypothesis to use the digitally searchable source of city directories. Searchable collections are available on Ancestry and Fold3, at least. The first step is searching one of those collections, possibly both if they contain different years. I would start by just searching the Ancestry collection and see what results I get. This would take less than an hour, maybe even a few minutes. The plan is quick to execute, and I'd rather complete it before spending time learning what years are included in each site's city directories. If a search of the one site reveals Frank in every year from 1932 back to 1919, checking another source is unnecessary. Instead, you'd select a different problem with a different hypothesis— this sub-problem is complete in that case.

The results of the plan will lead to a new plan. You don't need to worry about other sources for New York City directories at this point. If you had detailed knowledge of New York City directories that meant this would not be a hypothesis with a plan of one to five sources, you would create a different hypothesis. You create a plan based on your knowledge and experience, execute it and then decide if you need to learn more or do something else.

Don't Abuse This Shortcut

This example brings up an important point about making efficient choices, in this case, taking a shortcut. If you misuse this shortcut, it is a cheat, a very severe one for this particular problem.

Putting off learning what is included in a source is a modern option because searching with a search form can be so fast. If you had to use microfilm to research city directories, you would first have to identify what years were on which rolls. You would not just grab a roll and start using it. It might be for decades after Frank died or for years before the Frank Jones of interest could have appeared—before he was an adult or even before he was born. Occasional Genealogists, or any genealogist, should take advantage of the speed of online searching. That does not mean you can skip the more time-consuming steps pre-digital genealogists had to perform.

If your search revealed the Frank Jones you are interested in appears in every directory from 1919 until his death, great. You know you used the relevant directories. You know the man that died in New York City lived there while Jenni's ancestor was married to and having children with Liza in another state—you haven't been provided these details, but Jenni does know where Franklin lived in 1920, and it wasn't so close to New York City to cause an issue.

Jenni has no evidence that her ancestor was living a double life going back and forth to New York City from a distant state. Her cousins had just claimed the New York death for their ancestor based on the name and the fact Franklin was missing in other records. New York City was too far away for a man to easily live a double life there but not so far to exclude the New York man potentially being Franklin, Liza's husband.

In contrast, if your online search did not reveal Frank or only revealed him in some years, you need to determine if the missing directories are available in the source or collection that was searched. If they are, you want to verify Frank is not in them.

Searching using a form does not always work correctly. For this problem, it is vital to be sure if Frank appears in the directories or not. If he is in the directories, even though searching using a search form does not reveal him, that could mean New York City Frank is not the same as Jenni's ancestor Franklin T. Jones. This is not negative evidence, but the concept works the same. This time, not finding him doesn't give us information but leaves an alternative open. If Frank isn't in the directories, he could be the same man as Franklin. We need to be sure if he appears in the directories or not. Knowing he doesn't appear as a *search result* isn't enough.

You must verify what years are searched. For any searched years where he did not appear, you need to look at the images, if available, to verify he is not listed. If images aren't available, you want to try to find them for the years he wasn't found in to confirm he isn't listed. Searching online records is a quick first step, not your only step. This sub-problem is only helpful if certain years of directories are available and if we are sure whether Frank appears in those years. You can just check what is easy, but that may make this sub-problem useless because the information is incomplete.

A Word About Case Studies

This example showed how a sub-problem could be created for the main problem. Then a hypothesis could be created from that sub-problem. It is always difficult to provide examples for part of the research process because the existing and following research makes a difference. This is why genealogists love learning from case studies.

Case studies are real research that genealogists present for educational purposes. Articles in genealogy journals can be case studies. They can also be family histories which are not the same. Case studies help you understand the genealogy research process, not just read about a person or family— such as in a biography. Case studies can also be presented in lectures or in a course.

Part of the purpose of this book is to show what didn't work, which is difficult in a written case study. That's why examples are used instead of real case studies. Now that you know the advantage of learning from case studies, seek out journals so you can read them and attend lectures that present case studies. You can also get together with genealogy friends, in-person or online, and discuss your research and why you made the choices you did. I personally love doing this because everyone thinks a little differently. Even when people don't suggest new sources for you, hearing ideas from others helps you think differently and allows you to come up with new options.

Let's look at some more sub-problem examples. Seeing how Jenni could approach her Alford project will help you understand making good research choices. Often genealogists need to consider their options, much like how you see them through these examples.

Sub-problem Examples for the Alford Project

With Jenni's problem about Henry Alford, each source type she brainstormed could relate to a sub-problem or several. For example, "What religion was Henry raised in?" helps her determine which baptism or christening records to explore. "Did Henry own land as a young man?" helps her focus on deed records. The idea about marriage records for a Martha and a Mr. Alford could be used as a sub-problem exactly as Jenni listed it. For any of these sub-problems, several potential research plans could be created, *each plan testing one hypothesis.*

Below is a list of various sub-problems Jenni could work on related to her main problem of who Henry's father is. You can brainstorm sub-problem ideas. That is what this list represents. If you want to *use* a sub-problem, you need to apply the W-frame System to it.

Primary Problem: Who is Henry Alford's father?

Sub-problem ideas:

- Did Henry Alford own land as a young man, indicating he might have inherited it?
- What religion was Henry? Was he raised in this religion? Or, what religion was Martha, Henry's apparent mother?
- When did Martha Alford remarry? (This is based on an assumption but researching a sub-problem is often how you determine if the assumption is correct or incorrect, this is similar to testing a hypothesis because you're selecting the problem to determine its truth.)
- Does evidence exist Henry's father was living around the time Henry married?
- Research Henry's apparent half-sister. (This is not a specific question yet, it is just like starting research on any new person.)

Testable Hypotheses and Actionable Plans

We've examined how a question and a sub-problem differ from a hypothesis. Now it's time to deep-dive into options for creating a hypothesis and selecting a *good* hypothesis to test.

When creating a plan, your analysis should have provided you with one or more hypotheses to test. If you have no ideas, your analysis isn't done. Whatever problem you defined in pre-planning, whether it was your main problem or a sub-problem, you will be testing a hypothesis for that problem. You need to break your problem down to a hypothesis your research plan can test. You might want or need to break your problem into a sub-problem first.

We want to determine if our hypothesis is true or false. Prioritize completing the research process—going through all the steps of the Roadmap—over declaring a hypothesis true or false with just one plan, though. In the example about city directories for Frank Jones, it might be necessary to continue testing the same hypothesis in an additional plan that used another source to ensure all the necessary years were covered. Remember, in that example, my experience led me to believe the plan would quickly use one or two sources, which might cover all the years I needed. I didn't create a hypothesis I knew would require more than one plan to fully test.

If you knew more than one plan was necessary from the start, you would either adjust your hypothesis or the sources you planned to use before creating your plan. But as described in the New York City directories example, you can take advantage of quick-to-search online sources, learn more, and adjust your next steps. You don't want to leave a plan half-finished if you can help it. If it is unfinished, you did not create a summary or report, affecting future reviews. It might mean the results from that research get lost.

Actionable plans are plans you can easily finish. Remember, you can choose to end a plan so you finish the research process. If you still want to use some of the unused sources, simply add them to your notes or summary so you later create a new plan for those sources. Focusing on finishing the research process prevents things from getting lost, whether that is research results, your ideas, or even questions you have. But let's get back to creating research plans.

Creating a statement that can be tested as true or false isn't too hard. Instead of our sub-problem question, "What religion was Henry?" we create a statement, "Henry Alford was Southern Baptist." If you want to test that he was Southern Baptist, how many records will you need to check? You might find him listed as a Southern Baptist in the very first record you try. But what if you find fifty records you should check for the time and place Henry lived to be sure he doesn't appear in one of them? That could be a very large plan to complete.

This is where the rule about limiting the plan to between one and five sources comes in. That is between one and five individual records you will use, not one and five types of sources. Marriage records are a type of source. One book of marriages is one source—whether an abstracted and published book of marriages or the original court or church book.

The hypothesis, "Henry was Southern Baptist," doesn't have a natural division to decide which subset of records you'll use. This isn't a *good* hypothesis, although it is a hypothesis. In this case, treat this statement like a sub-problem and ask, "How will I solve this problem?" Determine which Southern Baptist records exist. Add limiting information to your hypothesis to make sure you have an actionable plan.

The limiting information could result in one of the following hypotheses:

- Henry belonged to a Southern Baptist church in Geneva County, Alabama.
- Henry's obituary appeared in the [Southern Baptist paper or papers that served Geneva County, Alabama]
- Henry belonged to a Southern Baptist church in Geneva, Covington, Coffee, Dale, or Houston County, Alabama, between 1880 and 1910.

Remember, when it is time to create the actual plan, you should have done the analysis, which included asking, "How can I solve this problem?" That means you should have learned what records exist for your problem. Try to select or craft a hypothesis that only requires you to use between one and five of those sources. If you are trying to create a plan and don't know what sources exist, treat your hypothesis like a sub-problem and go back to analysis and answer, "How can I solve this problem?"

Examples from Jenni's Alford Project

Before we get even better at research planning, let's go a little more in-depth on improving some sample hypotheses you saw in the initial chapter on research planning. We'll quickly review the basic hypothesis example you already saw.

> Who is the father of Henry Alford, born 10 December 1850 in Alabama and died 11 May 1913 in Geneva County, Alabama.

Here are some examples of types of hypotheses for this question:

- Robert is Henry's father.
- Samuel is Henry's father
- Henry's father died about two years before Martha had Henry's oldest known (possible) half-sister. Henry is listed as the heir of his father in probate records.
- Henry is listed as the son of his father in XYZ will book.

We considered the option of conflicting hypotheses—the first two. The final example was a hypothesis for a specific source you want to use. This can happen when you are researching the existence of sources for your problem. This is a little different from a true hypothesis you have come up with.

Let's first look at a hypothesis like this:

> Henry's father died about two years before Martha had Henry's oldest known (possible) half-sister. Henry is listed as the heir of his father in probate records.

Your hypothesis is worded this way because you think that is what happened. You formed a hypothesis you want to test instead of learning about a type of source you want to use.

This hypothesis has a timeframe based on the birth of the possible half-sister. That's why the information about her is included. This is a clue, and you turn it into a statement for your hypothesis. Use the timeframe along with a specific type of record to identify specific sources to use.

All About Hypotheses

If you can't test the hypothesis involving Henry's half-sister as true, you can easily alter it to test something slightly different such as:

> Henry's father died about four years before Martha had Henry's oldest known (possible) half-sister. Henry is listed as the heir of his father in probate records.

You don't have to look in the probate records you already used, so you decided to check the probate records for the two previous years. The fact you already used two years' records is part of the background information in your plan. This makes it very clear why you aren't using those records, in case you review this plan's Genealogy Roll-up but miss the previous plan's.

The hypothesis indicates obvious sources to check. This is a good hypothesis if your research leads you to think this is possible, of course. You might also keep the timeframe of the original hypothesis and consider a different type of source, or you could alter the location.

Don't Miss This

In this example hypothesis, the *where* wasn't stated, but you would have included it in a real hypothesis. It would have been the location of the probate records you wanted to check. The needed W-frame elements for the hypothesis are determined just like your problem W-frame elements. In this problem, research involving census records had been completed. Those records were what made it appear Martha

183

might be Henry's mother, and he might have a half-sister. Census records before and after the possible half-sister was born provide starting *wheres*. You might have had other information you used to select a *where* for the probate records, too. Just as with the main problem, if you can't define or estimate all the W-frame elements, you need to work on another project first to gather those details.

A hypothesis *is* a hypothetical situation, so you are free to use your problem's W-frame answers to narrow the *when* and *where* to different options for each hypothesis. You don't just have to use the W-frame elements from your problem as-is. You might decide the county immediately east of where you first find the potential half-sister in census records is the best place to start probate research. That uses the W-frame elements but not as-is.

You can even alter the *who* or *what* from the original problem because you believe that is a good hypothesis to test for the problem. In this example, the *what* is a relationship, the father. For a different problem, you might test a hypothesis where the *what* is an uncle or step-father because you want to test if a man that *might* be the father has a different relationship. For some problems, you could switch out the relationship of father for mother or even for a brother or sister. The options depend on the main problem you want to solve and the research you have done.

Your hypothesis is based on the selected problem. Both need the W-frame elements, but you can change them for the hypothesis because the hypothesis is not based on what is known to be fact. Remember, you are testing if something is true or false, so the W-frame elements in a hypothesis might be false. Test whatever statement you believe will help.

By creating a hypothesis, you are clearly recording your idea, what you are testing, and, therefore, what you are searching for. If you don't test the hypothesis, true, it is easy to adjust a hypothesis to something you think is the next most likely scenario. You don't have to be systematic by backing up the dates or working out from a location; you can test the options you think are most likely. Your plan records this so you know what you have tried by reviewing the summaries created after each plan was created.

> **Remember:** Record why you selected a hypothesis or sources as a part of every plan. This is a crucial element when you are not using your problem's W-frame elements as-is. *Why* reminds your future self the hypothesis is more like a guess, something you strongly believe is likely, or something in-between. Recording your *why* will keep you from being confused in future!

Use the Research Process to Your Advantage

If you are not using a systematic way to test options, you must ensure you're reviewing all relevant previous research, even if it happened the same day. Genealogists often mix up similar details as research progresses. Systematically working through your options is a technique to avoid misremembering things. But *you don't need to remember*; you take notes!

Few people have a detailed and precise enough memory to remember what is important when research planning. Many of us think we remember the details, though. We may remember details, but they might not be the right ones. Write things down and review what you write.

Pick a Hypothesis

You can brainstorm ideas for different hypotheses if you aren't sure which you want to start with or if you just want to get yourself thinking of hypotheses instead of questions. Brainstorming is creating a simple statement, so it isn't as time-consuming as creating an entire plan. When I say "brainstorm," I mean you'll think of ideas and put them in your notes. Write it down. Many ideas will be used later for this problem or perhaps as inspiration for a different problem. Sometimes even seeing your bad ideas helps. Just write it down so you can review it later.

> I've been intentionally vague with this last sentence talking about *it*. You could frame that sentence and hang it where you'll see it as you do genealogy. Not too long ago, I read an email newsletter that talked about brainstorming, specifically writing down your ideas. This wasn't genealogy related, but it is important for genealogists with too much in their heads. Once you write an idea down in a place you can review it, you can dismiss it from your brain. This helps you stay focused and feel less frantic. I often feel like swarms of ideas are flying around my head. The solution is to record the idea, but more importantly, it must be

recorded in a location you can find it again. Then you essentially let the idea go and get back to what you meant to be doing. This allows you to work faster. Now back to picking a great hypothesis from the ideas you recorded...

You don't just randomly create statements to test. These statements are based on analysis of previous research, that's why it's critical to review your past work. If you've ever thought, "Maybe so-and-so is the father," that's a hypothesis you can test. Something made you think that man was the potential father. Analyze why—think about what gave you that idea. Create a research plan. The information that gave you that idea is your background information, and your idea is the hypothesis. All you need to turn it into a plan is a short list of specific sources to use!

Recap:

- Your chosen hypothesis is based on the analysis you did in steps one through three of the Roadmap. That means it's based on the research you've already completed.
- Some problems need to be broken down into sub-problems before developing a narrow hypothesis to test.
- A good hypothesis leads to an actionable plan.
- An actionable plan is short, so you can complete it.
- As you're learning to research plan, just pick a hypothesis to start with. Don't get stuck trying to pick the perfect hypothesis.

Chapter 9:
Better Research Planning

"Gene, you've given me lots of ideas for how I could deal with my Alford problem. You said you knew what you would do, so what is it? Learn about his religion to use baptisms? Read deed books? Or do you have some source I haven't even thought of?"

Gene laughed. Like many genealogists, Jenni was trying to deep dive into research. Gene was never one for diving; too much pressure. "I'd go with the easiest option."

"What's that? I already searched all the websites I knew of. I thought I'd done all the 'easy' options."

"Almost. But come on, Jenni, tell me the easiest option for · your choices on that list."

> Henry Alford's death certificate
> ~~Henry Alford's birth certificate~~
> Henry Alford's baptism or christening record
> Wills for Alford men in ??? County, Alabama between ???
> ~~Tax records for _____ County, Alabama about ___?~~
> ~~(when Henry was 18-21)~~
> Marriage for a Martha and an Alford man in ???

> County, Alabama or nearby areas or along possible
> migration route.
> Deeds showing Henry got land from his father.

Jenni frowned at the list for a moment, then said, "Well, I guess it's the death certificate. But I'll have to order it from the state of Alabama."

"So?"

"I have to wait for it to come in the mail."

"So?"

Jenni stared at Gene. She didn't have a response.

Gene decided to spell it out. "Having to order one record, online, or even mailing in a form, when you have all the needed information, and even waiting for snail mail, doesn't make the research hard. It's just not instantaneous."

"OK," Jenni seemed to be thinking. Gene waited. Finally, Jenni asked, "So, should I do some of this other research while I wait?"

"I won't say you can't do the other research but a death certificate might list the name of Henry's parents. You don't have any other ideas that are simple. If you get the names of his parents, you might not need to do any of the research you're considering while you wait. It would be different if this was research you needed to do anyway. But researching his religion might be impossible. Personally, I wouldn't want to spend time on that until it was necessary or if I had a particular interest in it."

"Yeah, I see that. I wasn't sure if most of the research was relevant. They were potential ideas, but I didn't know if Henry's father left a will or owned land. I don't even know if Henry owned land. Maybe that's something I'll work on while I wait."

"That would be some research you probably want to do no matter the result of your death certificate request. You may not need to order the death certificate, or at least not right now. Abstracted Alabama death records are online. We can pull that up and see if a father is named. If so, you probably want to order a copy right away to make sure no errors were made in the transcription. But if the place for the parents' names is blank, you can wait to order a copy. It's up to you and probably depends on how much it costs or how easy it is to get. Some states make it hard to order a death certificate for genealogical use. I don't know about Alabama."

"Really? This information is online, and I haven't come across it?"

"Maybe you didn't recognize it for what it was. We don't know if you saw it since you didn't track your research."

"That's true." Jenni seemed to be having a realization. "Wow! That's a little scary. What else did I see and not recognize that would help me? I wish I had tracked my research. I'd love to review everything I found but thought wasn't helpful. It'd almost be like cheating. Using the research 'someone else' did for my ancestor. But that someone else is just a less experienced me."

"I know. I didn't do all this stuff when I was getting started, either. I don't want to think about what is lost to time, or at least what I won't find again for years. That's just depressing. Let's pull up that death record database and see if we can find Henry. Maybe we'll brighten up if we find a name for his father."

Gene and Jenni are going to try to find the death certificate abstract. In the following section, we'll look at improving your research process. Some of the examples will consider hypothetical situations based on whether Henry's death certificate lists a father's name or not.

***

You may still have several other questions about research planning, or worse, you don't have questions yet but will run into them as you try planning. This chapter covers topics related to research planning that can help take your plans from good to great.

We'll start with one question you might have come up with after finishing the last chapter. Which hypothesis do you or should you test first? Can you even decide that?

Which Hypothesis Should You Test First?

You have to use your judgment about what hypothesis to test first. Sometimes you have a strong idea of the answer to your question; test that hypothesis. Sometimes you have a few ideas; you must decide which hypothesis to test first.

Sometimes you have no idea what the solution is. In that case, you might have to create a research plan with a hypothesis for a source you want to check. An example is the hypothesis involving the will book, "Henry is listed as the son of his father in XYZ will book."

Jenni's idea for the wills was to identify the one will book for the time and place she believed Henry's father died. She might instead take that idea and create a similar hypothesis where she'd check up to five different will books. She doesn't know when or where the father died. She was hoping she'd have a good estimate. That would be a good hypothesis to test if she knew or could estimate the time and place to the point of picking one will book to use. Since she hasn't found that information, picking only one will book is probably not the best hypothesis to start with. The best hypothesis to test first is based on your problem and your past research. It isn't something you'll find stated in this book, in a blog post, or taught in a course.

Jenni's Best First Hypothesis

As Jenni's research stood at the start of this chapter, she should have one clear hypothesis to test.

> Henry Alford's death certificate lists the name of his father.

Jenni had one obvious source she should use, so her hypothesis didn't need to determine the father's name. As Gene pointed out, all the perceived necessary research for the other ideas might not need to be done at all. She might want to know what religion Henry is. Maybe that doesn't interest her and won't help her research. She had no evidence a will, probate records, or deeds for Henry's father might be found. Later she might discover such records, but the related hypotheses for those records aren't good options at this time. Whether Martha is Henry's mother and whether she remarried is probably of interest and helpful, but that wasn't directly related to the question of who Henry's father is. That would not be a good first hypothesis for the problem of who Henry's father is, although Jenni will likely do research related to those issues at some point.

There isn't one right way to decide what hypothesis to test first. The best way to decide is to start with the easiest testable hypothesis that might provide the answer to your main problem. In section three, you can learn how to prioritize which source to try first. This can be used for deciding which hypothesis to test first if you don't have a clear idea.

The One-Plan Rule

Considering what hypothesis to test first and what sources to use brings up a significant point you need to understand about planning research. Part of the reason we create small, easy plans is genealogists shouldn't create more than one plan at a time. This has been mentioned several times, but it is important enough to warrant repeating.

The results of a plan affect what the next plan should be. This "flowchart" element doesn't happen in the plan; it happens between creating plans. Jenni didn't need to spend weeks creating that huge plan for all those sources. She could spend weeks identifying all the possible marriage sources and all the possible deed books to check. But what happens when the third source provides new information that indicates it is pointless to check most of those locations?

The ideas Jenni came up with during the consideration phase, her ideas based on analysis, are helpful. These should be captured in notes, but it's not necessary to try to create a plan for each of them. At first, they are just ideas that live in your notes. With these ideas stored in your notes, you can add them to a plan once that seems like the next research you should do. Don't create a plan to store the idea; they are already stored safely in your notes, which you regularly review.

> **Important!** This "one-plan rule" applies to one problem. You can create as many plans as you want if they are for different problems. When it comes to creating plans for related sub-problems, ask yourself if the result of one plan could mean you wouldn't want to use the other plan.

Jenni's current plan is to check the online database of abstracted death records. As Gene mentioned, whether she immediately orders the death certificate even depends on the results of the plan. Certainly, what she does after that will depend on if a name is listed and what that name is.

The name could be common, like John Alford. It could be a name that seems uncommon, like Etheldred Alford. Jenni can likely find several John Alfords in Alabama; she would need to determine which one is correct. Only one Etheldred Alford might be found—or several, and with an uncommon name, they are likely related, which is an additional complication.

A name could be listed, and it might be even harder to deal with. What if the name listed has a surname other than Alford? That indicates Henry might be illegitimate, meaning he might not have any interaction with his father or that his surname was changed to Alford, possibly when he was adopted by a stepfather.

Before you do research, understand that all situations can have a variety of scenarios that will be best dealt with in different ways. Whether Henry's death certificate is found, whether a father is listed, and what name is shown all lead to unique next steps. Create one plan, so you only need to create the next best plan, not multiple potential plans, most of which you won't need.

Also, remember that you want to answer, "How can I solve this problem?" but you don't need to identify every single source that might help. You only need to create an actionable plan that you believe, based on your current knowledge, is the next best step.

You might have many sources you could use or just one. You might know most of the relevant sources or a very small percentage. It doesn't matter. You're not worried about how good your knowledge is. You obviously want it to be the best it can be, so you keep going through the research process. Instead of striving for perfection once, you keep improving each time. It's better to keep moving than stall. Although you want good knowledge and to make the best decision you can, the best decision always comes from progress over perfection. Sometimes progress is easy, and sometimes you need to make it happen. A perfect research order doesn't exist. Too many factors are involved.

***

Let's consider another hypothetical situation for Jenni. It's a pretty common situation, and you want to develop your skills for it.

Recognizing Conflict

Let's say Jenni has the death certificate with a name for Henry's father. And she has a family letter that gives a different name for Henry's father. These are potential answers to the main question, but they conflict. Each name is a hypothesis Jenni can test, one per research plan.

Once she found the death certificate and finished her research session, she needs to repeat the research process. She will do new analysis that integrates what she learned from the results of the research she just finished. During this analysis, she'll decide what sources can help her test her two conflicting hypotheses. She can refine her hypotheses if needed so they are small and actionable plans.

Finishing the research process and starting it again means taking your research results and reviewing them along with your past research. This is a chance to recognize a conflict if you didn't already realize it existed, such as if Jenni found the name on the death certificate but didn't remember about the family letter. Going back and reviewing what she already had, instead of just plunging into more research only based on the death certificate, changes the best next research options.

Don't Forget Why

Just as in note-taking, where *why* was tangled up with your search description and background information, why you are testing a hypothesis is tangled up with your background information for your plan. It doesn't have to be a separate item.

I intentionally give just three sections to the research plan because you should always have those three sections as separate items, the analyzed (W-frame) problem, background information, and plan.

You also need your hypothesis and have a clear reason for testing that hypothesis. You can put your hypothesis anywhere before your plan. Why you are testing that hypothesis must be apparent, but that might happen when you list your background information or in the way you define your problem. If it isn't clear, state it explicitly.

> **Tip**: As I do client work and make notes to myself, I've started listing hypotheses and my thoughts on why I have those hypotheses. I don't want this information to automatically appear in a client report, so previously, I didn't make these notes.
>
> However, I've found it extraordinarily helpful to state the hypothesis and then explain to myself why I formed that hypothesis. Often I either convince myself

it's a great hypothesis I should test as soon as possible or determine my logic is flawed, and that's clearly not the answer. Whenever you have a hypothesis, write it down, clearly marking it as a hypothesis so you don't think it's an uncited fact.

Explain, in writing, why you formed that particular hypothesis. This is just for you, so ask yourself questions if your thinking isn't completely clear. This can save you time if you decide not to use a hypothesis. Save your notes so you don't come up with the same flawed hypothesis again! It can also motivate you to do research that reveals itself as a great idea.

***

Let's go over the rules and best practices for genealogy research plans. We've covered some of these points across several chapters. I'll cover others in a moment. For now, start with the following:

- Create one plan at a time—keep ideas for other plans in your notes.
- One plan tests one hypothesis.
- Your hypothesis is for the problem you've chosen to work on; this might be a sub-problem to your main goal.
- Pick a hypothesis to test that you can test immediately or soon.
- Don't get bogged down in finding the perfect hypothesis; just get started.

***

Once again, here's a list of what needs to go into a research plan. You can add the parts to the note-taking template in a way you prefer, or you can just use this list as a reminder.

Every plan must include the following:

- One hypothesis to test
- Why you believe that hypothesis is important to test

The above two items can go anywhere in your plan before the list of sources.

The three sections of a plan are:

1. The single main problem and, if chosen, the single sub-problem (both need to be W-frame-defined)
2. Background information
3. List of exact sources you will use

These three sections make the most sense in the order given above. Leading with your W-frame-defined problem makes it clear when you review what that document is focused on so you know whether to even keep reviewing or move on to the next document.

Next Versus Now Research

You may need to explain why it's important to test that hypothesis next or now. These aren't the same thing. You may have research that clearly needs to be the next research done. In contrast, you might be testing a particular hypothesis *now* because you have access to the sources in your plan. This could be because you are on-site researching at an archive. It might be because you're paying for a subscription and will not be renewing it. As you're getting into doing great genealogy, you find yourself often explaining to yourself why you need to do specific research next. Many genealo- . gists in the transitional stage, where they aren't a beginner or advanced, shy away from recording things related to "why now" because it seems shallow or unprofessional.

Absolutely prioritize testing a hypothesis if you have a current paid subscription and don't want to renew it. Explaining why you made your hypothesis choice is even more important in this situation. Your future self won't remember the situation when that plan was made. Your future self might question your research skills if this isn't the best *next* research to do.

Genealogists are a judgmental group. We have to be. Genealogy is done by constantly judging the best decision to make. You should question if your past self made the right decision and how that affects the decision you are currently trying to make. Remind future self you know what you are doing!

All the information I've included about recording why, which is the top piece of information skipped in any stage of the research process, is about helping you correctly judge your past research. Own whatever stage you are in. Make it clear to your future self so she can deal with it appropriately.

Recap:

- Create short easy to complete plans.
- Test one hypothesis per plan.
- Create one plan (for one problem) at a time.
- Store your ideas for sources or plans in your notes.
- Don't get stalled worrying about the best hypothesis or plan to create.
- Use a template to make it fast to create a plan.
- Take notes on your plan to save time.
- Copy and paste to create a similar plan once you complete a plan.

Chapter 10:
A Little More about Reporting

"**H**orsefeathers!"

Gene gave Jenni a sidelong look, she wasn't sure what Jenni said, but she got the idea.

"OK, So the death certificate doesn't show parents' names. You've got plenty of other ideas."

Jenni grabbed the mouse, "Let's try those deeds."

"Uh, Jenni, why don't we finish the Genealogy Roll-up."

"I guess so." Jenni paused, "in fact, you're right. I could be here all night looking at deeds. I think I can come up with a better next idea."

"I'm sure you can. Before you look at a deed, you should see if you have any information indicating Henry even owned land."

"But don't I need to look at deeds to figure that out, anyway?"

"No. That's just one option. Some U.S. federal census records contain information about whether real property is owned or if the family home is owned. You also found that homestead record at some point which might have details about Henry's land ownership."

"Oh, yeah, I still haven't gone back to find that. I guess I should do some more review and finish using the sources I've already found."

"I think that's your best idea. And maybe you should try writing a report instead of just a summary."

"That sounds rather involved."

"It can be. The point is for you to combine lots of information together into one easy-to-read document. The great thing about doing your own research is you can create several easier and smaller reports and then review those to consolidate all the information into one report. It's still just summarizing what you've found, but with a report, you want details, particularly citing your sources. Your notes summary can be a short few sentences because the details are in your notes. But if you have ten sets of notes, you'd want to consolidate that into a report with more details than the ten summaries, but without it being as long as all the notes."

"I get it. Same idea, just summarizing more information for review."

"That's right."

Gene and Jenni discussed some options for "reporting to yourself." You can learn about these options in the next section.

***

At the end of section one, I reminded you to create a summary of your notes and also a summary of your review. The summary of a review session, that is, step three of the Brick Wall Solution Roadmap, is like a professional genealogy report. Learning to create a professional genealogy report, a report that will go to a client, is very helpful to your hobby genealogy work. At the same time, a professional genealogy report is overkill for what a hobbyist needs.

Important Definition

Source-cited: information that is source-cited has a footnote or endnote.

Maecenas lobortis in sem ut bibendum. Quisque placerat lacinia sapien, ut sollicitudin risus egestas non. Pellentesque molestie urna lacus, et elementum dolor dictum in.[6]

Cras a urna venenatis, hendrerit libero eu, gravida tellus. Curabitur in velit lacinia, varius ligula vitae, pretium justo.[7] Aenean mattis elit odio, vitae scelerisque ante blandit rhoncus.[8] Maecenas semper feugiat tellus.[9] Curabitur porttitor odio vel erat tristique sagittis.[10] Aliquam erat volutpat. Donec semper dui id augue rhoncus, in mattis sapien auctor. Curabitur au[...] venenatis faucibus.

---

[1] 1920 U.S. census, Bartow County, Georgia, population schedule, Adairsville District, Enumeration District (ED) 11, sheet 19 B, dwelling 361, family 363, Oliver McDaniel household; digital image, *Ancestry.com* (http://www.ancestry.com : accessed 13 September 2013); citing NARA microfilm publication T625, roll 235.

[2] Georgia Bureau of Vital Statistics, death certificate no. 150, Drewery Oliver McDaniel (1923); "Georgia, Deaths, 1914–1927," digital image, *FamilySearch* (https://familysearch.org/pal:/MM9.1.1/IDXL-YYD : accessed 13 September

Ex 1: Footnotes are listed at the bottom of the same page where the footnote reference number appears. The footnote reference is a super-script number at the end of the sentence. Multiple citations are combined under one footnote number. Numbers are not reused.

Proin viverra quam arcu. Morbi euismod ipsum erat, pellentesque mattis sapien vulputate ut. [1] Nunc cursus sem vitae lacinia ▸ ▰ntum. Donec aliquam placerat quam quis convallis. [2, 3] Sed quis lorem risus. Vivamus venen▰ ▰c gravida placerat. [4, 5, 6, 7] Ut augue magna, ultricies et molestie ac, adipiscing non mi▰ ▰ fringilla vulputate pellentesque. Phasellus vel urna scelerisque, vulputate nisl id, commodo orci. [8, 1] Morbi feugiat odio molestie dui ultrices mattis. Fusce mollis urna ac dictum interdum. [9] Quisque convallis pellentesque dapibus. Curabitur sit amet volutpat eros, eget ullamcorper nisi. [10] Nullam eget bibendum sem. [11, 12, 2]

Ex 2: Endnotes are provided after the text as a single list of numbered sources, one citation per number. The endnote reference appears in brackets at the end of the sentence. Multiple endnotes can be listed and the numbers are reused.

Often in genealogy, you only hear about footnotes. It makes it sound like that is your only option. I use the phrase "source-cited" because citing your exact source is what is important, not whether you use footnotes or endnotes. **Note:** There are a variety of rules to choose from when formatting footnotes or endnotes. The example images show common scenarios for genealogy reporting. When reporting to yourself, a "correct" format is not something to worry about. If you are publishing your work, including writing reports to clients, you should learn standard formatting for your situation or publication.

If you aren't comfortable creating formal, formatted citations, which are abbreviated, endnotes may be your better option. I personally prefer endnotes even in my professional reports because they give you an advantage in a review. The same endnote is reused for the same source, unlike footnotes. Just by looking over the endnotes cited in your report, you can see if you've relied on a variety of sources or just one or two. Endnotes can be a better option for reports to yourself for both reasons but source-cited information is what is most important, not format.

Besides source-cited information, you might also refer to the source in the text, making it clear what source provided the information. This is not source-cited but inline. An example of an inline source is, "Henry's death certificate did not list his father." A previous sentence would have cited the death certificate, meaning the full details of the death certificate are provided. You cannot write an entire understandable report by using inline sources only. The footnote or endnote will contain many more details than you could clearly reference inline.

Citing Source and Formatting Citations

Because we're talking about reports, conventions for writing a professional client report exist but aren't necessarily valid for reports to yourself. Some conventions lead to a better report, and others only lead to a better report when given to another person, such as a client. I'm not going into these conventions because it can be confusing to explain the options.

The vital part to understand is that following some conventions means the only clear way to cite your sources is through source-cited sentences. A report to yourself needs to have clear sources, but hobbyists still learning to write reports sometimes use options that make their sources clear but are not options a professional should use. This can cause a disconnect between the information you might read about the proper way to write a report and what you are doing. Many rules and best practices don't apply to reporting to yourself. You do need to know when to use source-cited information or not, though.

All genealogists need to cite their sources when explaining what they've done. Professional genealogists use standardized citations to ensure the client and anyone else receiving the report can understand those citations. Standardized citations don't take up as much space, making the report easier to read.

You don't have to use standardized or formatted citations for your own use. It's more important to include source-cited information, even if you must write out a longer but unformatted citation to get this done. Perfect citations are for professionals. You need the same source information, and possibly more, in your summaries, notes, and reports, but don't get hung up on the format.

"Attaching" Citations in the 21st-century

Your citations need to be "attached" to the report or whatever document you are writing. When we used paper, this meant physically attached. Professionals needed to bind the pages with the citations to the pages with the text. Footnotes appear on the page with the text, so this wasn't as big a deal. If you use endnotes, as I do, this would have meant stapling or binding the report somehow.

Digitally, the citations need to be in the same file. That means you can't have a separate document where your sources live. This can be tempting, so you can reuse it without recreating your citations. This is a good time-saver. Instead, copy and paste the citations you need into your text document or link them so they appear in the text document. Remember, this is a rule for reports or summaries, not for every type of genealogical material we might create. If possible, keep the sources in the file with your work but this might be too difficult. For example, you might be doing analysis using a map and need your sources in a separate file due to the software you are using. When you write your report based on that analysis, everything will be brought together in one report file.

Tip: Even if you work digitally, others might print what you share with them. A good practice is numbering your pages, including the total number of pages. I once had an institute organizer pass my digitally submitted pre-institute homework to my instructors without the pages with my bibliography. Their initial suggestions duplicated the sources I had already used. I was not happy, but I learned my lesson about numbering pages. I use "page x of y" in my footer, where x is the current page number, and y is the total number of pages.

Explain It to Me, or Rather to You

Professional reports also go to a different person than who wrote the report. The professional tries to explain anything the client needs to know. Hopefully, the professional knows a lot more than the client, so they will explain basic things, sometimes even genealogy basics you and I have known since we started.

You should explain anything to your future self that she may not know. This can be something you might forget or that you had to work out during your review or analysis. That's why reviewing and writing down what you found is so important. You do not need to explain to your future-self things that are beyond obvious to you. This is personal based on your own knowledge and experience.

Easy on the Eyes

Professional genealogy reports also need to be easy to read. You also need this. Because a professional gives the report to someone else, the format must be universally easy to read. In a report to yourself, you can indulge your own whims to a certain degree. If you like your text in dark green, go for it. Light pink text? Maybe not. I am positive all of us are aging, and what seems easy to read today may not be easy to read in ten or twenty years. Make your report easy to read for your future self, who will have older eyes.

Related to ease of readability is a professional's choice when branding their report. Some professionals prefer a basic report, and others prefer something branded. Branding a report means using specific colors and fonts, possibly even graphics such as those found on printed letterhead.

You can do this if you wish. Using graphic elements is attractive. But realize if you see this, you're likely looking at examples of professional reports; that look isn't necessary when you report to yourself. I *need* my professional reports to be heavily branded. I've just got this thing about colors and style.

Before I was a professional, I always got tripped up trying to get my personal reports to look like the examples I saw. I spent way too much time worrying about formatting reports to myself. Not only did this worry waste a lot of time, but it also resulted in paralysis when it came time to report. Don't let this happen to you! Remember, you can think of a report as a summary or review notes if that simplifies the concept so you get it done.

Cite Yourself

Here's one thing that you may need to add to your report to yourself, though. You want it to be clear what notes your report is based on. When working for a client, information is often copied from notes into the report.

This is because professionals often don't provide their original notes. I would never recommend a professional provide their original notes. It costs the client more money as the professional would work slower to ensure the notes did not contain anything the client shouldn't see. An example would be my suggestion of recording your hypothesis ideas and why you came up with them. These sometimes turn out to be "dumb ideas," and you tell yourself that in your notes. It saves time to recognize a dumb idea before it's tested with a plan, but I don't want it preserved in a client report!

Notes should be for the researcher. As a professional, I find my client gets the best results when I write the notes for myself, and I always take my personal notes this way. Ethically, a professional should put anything relevant from their notes into the report. They should also ethically exclude all the fluff or chaff the client doesn't need. This is not the same when you are both researcher and client, which is the situation for your personal research.

If you create your report like review notes, the source, as called for in the notes template, is the notes you reviewed. You should source-cite any facts to the individual sources if it is unclear. I recommend two general formats your report could follow. This will affect how likely it is you need to source-cite individual pieces of information.

Professional reports, format two in the following section, is a narrative report like a family history is a narrative. The researcher explains the results, not the research process, narratively. This means working through the information found in chronological order. If you've used multiple sources, this probably means you will source-cite one source and then another as you move through the information chronologically.

In contrast, the first format is easier to get started with. It uses the same notes template you are already familiar with. In your notes, you use one source, listing all the information it supplies. Then you use another source and show the information it supplies. This is like two different sections. All the information in one section is from one source, so you don't have to source-cite each individual piece of information.

Below is an outline of each format. You can use this to alter your notes template to a review template. Alternatively, you can use your favorite outline to create a report template of your own.

Report Format 1: "Review Notes" Style

- Date of the review
- Problem/Why/Backgournd/Etc.

Describe the specific problem, including why you are reviewing the specific notes. This could be all the notes related to the problem or only specific notes, make sure this is clear. Don't forget to include any relevant background information for when you review this report in the future!

- Summary of findings

As with other notes, this is added after the review is complete. You may need to source-cite individual facts or refer to the following notes.

- First set of notes you reviewed ("Section 1")

Include enough details someone else could find these notes within your files. How this works depends on how you store and organize your notes. *This is the citation to your notes.*

- Section 1 Text

After the citation to the first set of notes you are reviewing, make your notes. If the set of notes refers to *one* source, that source should be clear in the citation you listed above. That means you would not need to source-cite any individual facts. All facts come from that single source.

If your notes were from several sources, you might choose to list each source and the information it provided or source-cite individual information, your choice.

- Section 2 Citation

Include the citation to the second set of notes you are reviewing.

- Section 2 Text

Add your current notes from the review of the second set of notes.

- Section 3 for the third set of notes

And so forth. Your summary appeared before these sections, so no conclusion is needed at the end.

Report Format 2: Narrative Report (or "Professional Style")

- Date of the review
- Problem/Why/Etc.

Describe the specific problem, including why you are reviewing these particular notes, just as with the review notes format. You likely do *not* need to include background information, as it will be in the body of the report.

- Summary of findings

Added after the review is complete. You should not need to source-cite individual information, as it will be cited in the following narrative section.

- Report (Body)

You will describe in detail what you have found from your review. This section includes any information, conclusions reached, and analysis done. If you have a lot of research, this is often similar to a person's individual history, but it depends on what your problem is.

For very specific problems, especially before they are solved, this might be a discussion of the information found and how it relates to each other, including conflicting information.

**

For either of the formats above, you can also add a section with questions or next actions if you wish. I put questions, tasks, action items, or other items before the body. During future reviews, I want to see these easily.

Choosing Your Format

The second format is much more powerful when you need to do a lot of analysis, but it is also much harder to learn to do when it doesn't sound like a story of someone's life. Because this report is for you, use whatever format works for you and work on improving this skill.

Reporting is one skill that requires practice more than education. You want to learn about reporting, writing, and analysis, but the knowledge will not stick until you regularly practice. Because of this, I haven't covered reporting in more depth in this book. Most genealogists I've worked with through the blog have never tried reporting. Often when they send me an email describing their problem, it's the first time they've written it all down. And most of them have been doing genealogy for over a decade.

I would far rather see you trying to report than focusing on reading about how to report.

Here's another one of my cheats, yes, a cheat, not a shortcut, for when reality gets in the way of your best intentions. You need to cite your sources. However, if even getting a description of what you've found seems a monumental task, just focus on writing down what you've found. Then come back to that same narrative and work on adding in citations.

Keep working on it. If you can't write *and* include citations, add the citations later. But make it a priority to add those citations! Because excluding citations is a pretty big cheat and a very serious one, I encourage you to push pause on any other genealogy until you get those citations added. Don't get distracted doing new research. Don't avoid the citations by working on a different problem. Spend your genealogy time adding citations to that report. You can edit and update the report but don't let the citations just slip away because they're hard to add. Creating citations isn't much fun. Accept it and create them anyway.

> **Tip**: Many online research sites now provide a citation. These citations often miss key components you should include, but better to copy and paste that citation into your notes, reviews, and reports rather than leaving the citation out completely. Genealogists can be perfectionists, so if you don't like how those provided citations look, get over it if it's the difference between a citation and no citation. I don't like them either, but it's better than nothing. If you think those

citations are great, find time to compare them to how a citation of that type is created using a standard guide such as *Evidence Explained.*

Now here's a shortcut to go along with this cheat. Part of the reason you want to add citations is you can then reuse any or all of your report as appropriate. This will save you a huge amount of time adding citations to a future summary, report, or notes. What is a report today may be background information for your next plan.

Writing up your results and reporting, regardless of whether your problem is solved or not, helps you pull everything together. It's vital to genealogy success. Good, better, and best ways exist to report to yourself. At least get started doing it. You can keep building this skill, and you will find what works best for you.

Recap:

- Reports for yourself share some characteristics with professional genealogy reports but not others.
- Make your report easy to read but don't worry about giving it a certain look. You can use formatting and graphics, like you'd see on printed letterhead, or you can keep it simple.
- You need to cite your sources, but they do not need to be formatted.
- Your sources, above all, need to be clear. This means it needs to be clear which source provided which piece of information. Traditionally, genealogy reports

use footnotes for this. Endnotes are an alternative to footnotes.

- You may not need footnotes or endnotes if you use a report format that lists what information came from each source. This will look like your note-taking template.

- If you decide to write a narrative report, you will need to use footnotes or endnotes. Footnotes often need to be formatted to save space. Endnotes don't have this limitation when you're reporting to yourself.

- Report or write up your results even if your problem isn't solved.

- It is better to write up your results and not cite your sources than skip writing. However, try to add citations to your report. You can then reuse the citations or even report text as you continue to review and report.

Bonus: More about Writing an Analysis

I promised back in chapter six I'd briefly talk more about writing an analysis once you knew more about reporting. If you remember, the word analysis is used as both a noun and a verb in genealogy. Most of chapter six was about the verb but there were a few more items related to the noun I wanted to include.

A report can contain an analysis along with other written information or only be an analysis. Genealogists preserve the results of analyzing in reports whether they are called an analysis, a report, a proof argument, or any other name.

Remember, your analysis—the verb—is not complete until you write an analysis.

Yes, You Must Write

Providing something besides a written explanation, such as a chart, timeline, map, list, or table, is an in-between or in-progress piece of information. If you've ever had the experience where someone shows you a chart or spreadsheet and says, "This explains everything," without explaining verbally or textually, you've experienced the in-between stage of analysis. A chart, graph, spreadsheet, etcetera does not explain anything. It shows data. You have to think about what that data means.

A pie chart of your monthly spending can show you spend 10 percent on eating at restaurants and 50 percent on rent. That's data. What you probably want to know is if the money spent in each area is reasonable or is something that needs to be modified. The chart alone doesn't give you the answer. You have to have a specific question and consider how that information relates to that question.

Thinking is analysis. In genealogy, a written analysis explains the question and what you thought so someone else can follow your reasoning. That someone else might be your future self.

A written analysis can be simple, or it can be extremely complex. If you did the analytical work to reach a conclusion, you can write the analysis. If that was simply thinking about how the information leads to that answer, that is what you explain in writing. If it involved other types of analytical work or tools like charts and maps, you have to figure out how to summarize that work and information in sentences. You did the work, so you can write the analysis, even if you have to practice to get good at it.

Use whatever tools you need to analyze, such as charts, maps, and tables. Pulling data and putting it in a chart is breaking your problem down, as is picking one question related to your problem and answering it in writing. Various tools or methods work best for different problems and genealogists. Use what helps you.

You need to write your final output in sentences, although you may include some of the tools to support it. Writing an analysis puts the pieces you broke down back together. If paragraphs are causing you too much trouble, try to explain the results of your analysis with bullet point sentences. Keep working on being able to explain your analysis in coherent paragraphs, though. Aim for progress over perfection. That means give it a try. Do your best and practice.

One warning: a genealogical analysis cannot be automatically generated. It can be automatically *compiled* from statements you enter in your genealogy software explaining your reasoning, but the computer can't do the reasoning. With that said, I would actually consider compiling all your analyses a cheat. The mental process that takes you from ideas to a coherent paragraph, not just random statements, is important. You may struggle to write an analysis because you need to do more analyzing or research. This is another way the genealogy research process helps you do better work. When we skip writing a conclusion, we can either think our problem is not solved when it is or is solved when it is not.

Either way, you're wasting your time selecting next steps if you are wrong.

Writing your results in coherent paragraphs is an important part of genealogy. Even compiling pre-written sentences into paragraphs partially breaks this process, especially if you are writing an analysis.

With that said, you can absolutely save your analysis (the paragraphs) and reuse them to compile a complete report. This is different because you did the thinking work of creating paragraphs. Selecting which paragraphs provide all the information for a report is what's important for the report. That is equivalent to putting the sentences together into paragraphs, but you're putting paragraphs into coherent sections. It is a great shortcut to reuse your already written paragraphs to create reports focusing on different parts of your research.

This distinction may not be obvious to you now. The more you report, especially reporting after reviewing multiple sets of notes or reports, this starts to become more and more obvious. If you already have experience reporting, start saving time by reusing analysis or other reporting paragraphs. In this situation, you don't need to reinvent the wheel. However, that wheel is unique to your research so you must invent it the first time by writing coherent paragraphs. Once you've done that, you can put it on any vehicle, a report, you need it for.

Section 3: A Few More Essential Skills

Chapter 11:
Genealogists Love Clues

Jenni had asked Gene to show her an example of how to create a simple report. Gene gave Jenni some reports from her own research, but they were more involved than Jenni felt she was ready to create.

"Gene, can't you show me a simpler example?"

"I'm not sure, Jenni. Honestly, I'm just like you, but a few years farther down the research road. I have plenty of old research I haven't reviewed, so I have plenty of research where I don't have reports. I've focused on updating a few projects I'm most interested in. Why don't we try going over what you're finding too complicated."

"OK, we can try."

Jenni scowled at Gene's report she had printed. "Honestly, it makes me feel kinda dumb. I'm not sure I understand some of the words you used." She paused for another bout of scowling. "And I don't quite understand how you figured this out." She shook the two-page report. More scowling and some forehead rubbing followed. "Or maybe, because I don't understand some of the words, I don't see how you got from A to B. Or is it A to Z? I'm just confused."

Gene took the report to refresh her memory of what example she gave Jenni, "Hmmm. Maybe this example was a bit more advanced. But I think we can work through this. In fact, this is a great example of using clues."

"Well, I feel clueless."

"That's probably how many people feel when they see these clues. But genealogists need to love learning about new kinds of clues and how to use them. Great genealogists love clues. Let's talk about clues and evidence before we get into how I determined this death date from a bunch of tax records and incomplete probate records. But also, remember, this is a report I wrote to myself. I wrote it the way I'd understand it. I didn't write it for anyone else. This wasn't the best report to share. I remembered it was a problem where reviewing everything I had done made a huge difference. That's why I shared it with you. I didn't mean to confuse you. Sorry."

Learn some basic clue-related definitions and why geneal-ogists need to love clues in the next section.

***

Before diving into clues, let's brush up on some basic genealogy terms.

A "source" is anything that provides genealogical infor-mation. It is a source of information. An equally important word to understand is "evidence." Evidence is information related to the question we are trying to answer. Different kinds of evidence exist in genealogy, but that is a more advanced topic for a different book. If you are reading a genealogical article or other educational information and see a description of the type of evidence, it's probably important. You can search the internet to learn more about types of genealogical evidence when you're ready.

Important: A source is anything that provides information, not something that provides an answer or provides evidence. "Information" and "evidence" are two distinct words in genealogy for a reason.

Here's another distinction to consider as well, the difference between clue and evidence.

This book has used the word *clue* and even *hint,* which is the same thing. *Clue* does not have a genealogical definition. Some clues are evidence, and some are clues to something besides the question you are trying to answer. The word evidence has a definition in genealogy—and clue does not— for a reason. Not all clues are evidence. Clues are hints of *something*. Evidence is information related to the problem you're trying to solve. Evidence doesn't exist without defining our problem. Clues are everywhere. We have to recognize them to use them, but we can capture clues without recognizing them as clues.

A *clue to the answer* is evidence. When your question changes, a clue can become evidence. That's why I like to think about clues. If you capture a clue, you've captured potential evidence. A clue to another source to check is not evidence, but you still want to pay attention to it. If you're lucky, you might uncover a clue that is a map with a giant X on it pointing to the lost family Bible. The Bible might be something you want, but unless your question is, "Where is the lost family Bible?" the map is not evidence. Genealogists want clues, not just evidence.

A clue isn't an answer, but it can point you toward an answer. Not all clues are obvious or obviously valuable to you. Focusing only on finding the answer can leave you stuck or maybe just leave you missing the map to the lost family Bible. Even focusing solely on evidence can be problematic. Tons of clues exist in the millions of available sources. You'll find very few answers. Even with evidence, you might miss the evidence you'll need tomorrow if you only focus on what is evidence for today's problem.

Why You Need Information, Not Just Answers

If you've only been focused on finding sources with answers, make a mindset shift—start thinking about finding and keeping information. You learned to do this in the chapter about taking great notes. You want to capture clues, but you might not recognize them yet. By capturing information, you'll capture the clues without needing the experience to know what is a clue and what isn't. Also, "useless information" can suddenly become a clue when you find new information. That's why it's so important to take good notes that capture *information*.

Once you've captured information, you can identify and use *evidence* for the question you are trying to answer. This strategy captures information, and as your evidence recognition skills grow, your genealogy will improve. The biggest advantage is that you already have information when you have a new question. It may be evidence for the new question.

That means you may already have evidence without doing any new research!

Remember, evidence is related to the question you are trying to answer. Your question can change, so whether a piece of information is evidence can change. Compare this to only capturing answers, not information. If all you capture are answers, as your skills grow, you won't have information that contains potential evidence. You only have the same answers you had before.

What a difference.

We want clues because:

- Evidence is a clue to an answer. Most genealogy solutions come from putting evidence together, not from finding *the answer*.
- Clues can be a clue to something besides a solution, like another source we can try, or anything else, such . as where the family Bible is hidden.
- Clues (information) can become evidence when your question changes.

And don't forget, information can become clues when our skills or knowledge increases.

Capturing the Most Clues

Using a variety of sources provides the most clues. Genealogists never know where they will find an important clue. We make decisions to use the low-hanging fruit first.

Low-hanging fruit refers to sources that are easy to use and likely to provide an answer to our question. We'll look at this a little more closely in the next chapter.

The phrase *low-hanging fruit* is appropriate because, just as in a fruit tree, you'll find more fruit of varying levels of difficulty once you use the low-hanging fruit. Your problem might not have the lowest-hanging fruit possible. Most problems have something you'd find worth picking, though. The more fruit you pick—that is, sources you use—the harder it gets to get more sources and information. The fruit is higher-hanging, but it is still there. Remember that most problems require we find clues and then compile evidence to come to a solution. Usually, problems are not solved by picking a source and immediately finding the answer we wanted. Even when we get an answer, you want to be sure it's correct, which means using more sources to verify what you found. We want to gather as many clues as possible to give us the best chance of success.

We need to use as many relevant sources as possible. Identifying and using sources increases the chance of finding a vital clue for the problem you're working on. But as you do this, you'll also find clues you'll use for other problems. But only if you take notes that capture the information and then review your research.

When you review, you recognize more or different clues, including evidence for a different problem. Reviewing also allows you to recognize conflicting evidence if you don't realize it while researching. Using various sources, taking notes, and reviewing helps with your current genealogical problem and makes future problems go faster. You've already learned about taking notes and reviewing. In a later chapter, you'll learn Gene's method for coming up with source ideas.

As a reminder, review your research before doing extra work to find new sources. You want to use the clues you already have first. Jenni has gone over everything she has already found for her Alford problem. Of course, she didn't track her past research or take notes, so she can't be sure of what she did. She has tried to remember what she can. She's also gone back and taken notes from the sources she does know she's used. That means she's already captured clues from those sources before trying to find new sources.

One clue she had was a picture of Henry's tombstone from Find-A-Grave. This picture provided the clue that led her to Henry's death certificate. The death date on the tombstone indicated Henry died once death certificates were kept in Alabama. The clue suggested that a death certificate should exist. The information on the tombstone didn't answer Jenni's question about who Henry's father was. It isn't even evidence for that question. But, it did provide a clue to a new source and one that might solve Jenni's problem.

Unfortunately, the death certificate didn't provide an answer to her problem. It didn't provide evidence for her problem, either, because it didn't provide information directly related to her problem. Clues might still be found in the death certificate.

Clues in a death certificate can include a social security number. That's a clue to records from the Social Security Administration. Unfortunately, Henry died before Social

Security was established, so that's not a clue Jenni found. Death certificates can indicate someone was a veteran, which is a clue to military records or even evidence for a problem asking about military service. The place of burial can be a clue not just for where they were buried but other information, such as their religion. A residence listed on a death certificate can indicate new places to research. Other names found on a death certificate can be new people to research. Even a cause of death or the person who reported the death can be used as clues. Clues, not just evidence, can appear in many forms and can often be used in multiple ways. Genealogists need to love clues.

Chapter 12:
An Orchard of Sources

"Gene, you've got me pretty excited about using clues now. But I had a thought while we were looking at your report, and I've had this thought while trying to create research plans, too." Gene indicated Jenni should go on. "How did you decide which sources to start with? You used some things I hadn't considered. I see now how important they were for clues, but before you explained this, they seemed useless. How did you know what to use?"

"That's not a simple answer, Jenni. The easy answer is genealogists shouldn't ignore any source. For this problem," Gene nodded at the report, "I was so desperate I wasn't planning so much as using anything I could get my hands on for that time and place. Any source I could find for that county in the 1850s, I looked at it. Sometimes you get to that point, but that's not where you start."

Gene tapped her pen on the report as she considered how to answer Jenni's question better. Jenni waited. She had gotten used to seeing Gene ponder the best way to explain the intricacies of family history research before speaking.

"I don't think I can answer how I decided which sources to start with for this report. When you have a truly hard brick wall, you use whatever sources you can find for the specific sub-problem you're working on. But you need to work through the available sources before reaching that point. I can explain the criteria I use in general when I have many sources I could possibly use. If I have too many hypotheses to consider, I can use the same criteria to decide which plan to create first, too."

Gene took a breath. Jenni knew that meant she was about to try to emphasize a point. "There's one thing I want to emphasize." Jenni laughed to herself over picking up on Gene's pedantic tells. "This is all about common sense. My cousin taught me this because I was trying to use some complicated, convoluted system to decide which research plan to create. I had this crazy weighted score system I came up with. It seemed reasonable when I created it, but in retrospect, it was a waste of time. For whatever reason, genealogists either ignore most of their available sources or think picking a place to start needs to be a production. It's just common sense. If even after learning these easy considerations you're stalling over what source to use, just pick one and start."

Learn the common sense criteria for deciding which sources to start with.

***

When first talking about altering the notes template into a planning template, you were given some considerations to use to narrow your problem so you could create an actionable plan. Those were a simplified variation of what this chapter covers. This isn't a hard concept to learn, but one too many genealogists skip. Let's dive a bit deeper into selecting sources when you have many to choose from.

Previous chapters mentioned *low-hanging fruit,* which is where this chapter's orchard reference came from. I've heard the *low-hanging fruit* term used in reference to genealogy sources several times, and it resonates with me, so I'm also using it, hoping it'll be easy for you to remember.

Before we get too far into this, always remember you start with the *low-hanging fruit* because that just makes sense. We don't ignore the rest of the orchard! Genealogists often lean to extremes. One only uses *low-hanging fruit* and says they're stuck when that doesn't solve their problem. Another skips the *low-hanging fruit* because it doesn't meet their exacting and unreasonable standards for high-quality sources.

Ideally, genealogists use common sense. Start with the *low-hanging fruit*. Don't stop with it. Also, *low-hanging fruit* is a phrase related only to the ease of access and use of a source. We're going to go over those criteria in a moment. A source is classified as low-hanging fruit before you get it and use it. The phrase has nothing to do with evidence evaluation. Genealogists that skip *low-hanging fruit* sources usually do so because they aren't "good sources." That is a different topic; you can read about it in this post: https://bit.ly/source-correct.

In summary, there's no such thing as a *good source*. Genealogists do perform source evaluation, but you have to access a source and see what information is in it first.

Use common sense; *low-hanging fruit* can provide clues, including clues to other sources. An easy-to-get source might provide questionable information, but that information might be a clue to getting a source with high-quality information. In that case, it made the second source *lower-hanging fruit* than it initially was. Why wouldn't you take advantage of that?

Identifying Low-hanging Fruit Sources

When all else is equal, you'll use four source characteristics when deciding which source to explore first. You can use these considerations to prioritize your use of sources or to help you decide between hypotheses. These are great considerations to apply when trying to knock out genealogy tasks—see Chapter 14, "Is It a Problem?"

Four Source Considerations

Low-hanging fruit means a source is easy to use. Here are four considerations to think about when choosing what to use:

- A source that should give you the information you are seeking, your *answer,* versus providing evidence or clues.
- A source that is easy for you to access.
- A source that is easy for you to use once it is accessed.
- A source you can understand.

These considerations are not binary, easy or hard. They offer a range, and within each is its own range. A source might give you a partial answer, be free to access but involves a fifteen-minute drive from home, and is not searchable—which means not the easiest to use. You might understand the source in general but not perfectly. I'd go get that source.

Keep in mind I specifically stated "for you" because your knowledge, skills, and personal needs are part of this. If we viewed these considerations as four sliders, you'd want to start with sources where most sliders were to the left. You would then continue using sources with sliders progressively farther to the right. As long as a source is related to your problem, you want to consider it.

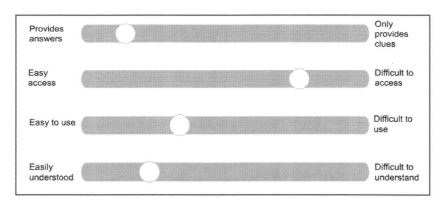

This is always a tricky topic to try to explain because it is a sliding scale and personal to you. Consider these other points, too:

- Some sources are relevant to your problem because they provide clues to other sources instead of evidence for your problem.
- A source can be inaccessible to you right now, but this can change.

What is Source Access?

When considering source access, it can mean a source you directly access, like viewing it online or visiting a repository to personally use it, or it can mean a source someone else gets for you. Jenni ordering the death certificate from the state of Alabama is an example. She could also call a cousin in Alabama and ask him to get a copy for her. She could see about hiring someone to get a copy for her.

Online research gets us used to the idea of directly accessing sources. In the past, most genealogists had to use someone else to get access to a source. This was often done via mail. Research trips were the best way to do a lot of research for yourself, though. Don't overlook other ways to access records.

Ease of access involves your budget, your time, your mobility, your internet speed, where you live, and even your preferences. I hate driving. I would use microfilm near me before I'd drive two hours to search online, especially if I suspected using the microfilm would take less than two hours. But I'd have to choose a two-hour drive over a trip to Europe to do research. Neither my budget nor my time would allow the overseas trip.

Occasional Genealogists are primarily limited by their time; that's what makes them Occasional Genealogists. I would probably have to skip research involving a two-hour drive simply because I'm too busy writing this book to take the time for that research. Depending on your situation, you may also incorporate how soon you can access a source as part of ease of access. When you're creating a research plan, you want to perform that research soon. Otherwise, you might do related research that requires you to alter the plan. You will need to decide what "soon" means for you, and it likely depends on how often you get to do genealogy.

Situations exist where you want sources you can't access now but know you can access later, such as knowing you'll visit a location in the future. Use your common sense, not a hard and fast rule. *Soon* is important when creating a research plan but requires your judgment.

The next chapter goes into four ways to develop ideas for other sources. It incorporates the issue of access. Anytime you think about sources, consider all four criteria, as well as if a source exists in other ways. Other ways can be access methods or physical sources that are copies of the same source.

A source might be online at multiple sites. A source exists in its original format but could be on microfilm—do multiple repositories have the microfilm? A source might have been abstracted into a published book. A source might only exist in its single original, offline format, but you might have three of four ways to get a copy.

Also, consider how easy a source is to use and ways around any issues. Records in a foreign language you don't speak are not easy to use. They may also be harder to access. Can you hire one person to get you a copy and translate the copy for you? You can find genealogists that offer this service at a reasonable price. What is a reasonable price varies based on your budget, but it's always cheaper than making an international trip yourself and finding you're unable to read the record!

Even as a professional, I've hired another professional with specialized knowledge of certain sources to do select research for me. They had better access to the sources I wanted and expert knowledge in using those sources. It would have cost my client a lot more if I had tried to do that same research directly or even gotten copies and figured out all the intricacies the expert knew off the top of his head. Considering a cost like this applies to your own research as well. If you don't understand what a source is telling you, you might have just missed the answer. Although you always have a next step, at least to verify a direct answer, what you do next differs depending on recognizing you've found the answer versus thinking you found nothing or, at best, some clues.

Use your common sense in the genealogy source orchard. Always start with the *low-hanging fruit*. Use *low-hanging fruit* even if you think it's not very good quality. This isn't actual fruit but a source. It might provide a clue that makes another source more accessible to you. It's more like a video game where grabbing the right low-hanging apple gives you a grappling gun or a ladder, not just an apple. Using online family trees is often the *lowest-hanging fruit*. You may not be able to determine if the information provided is good quality, but you can use them for clues.

Chapter 13:
More Sources

It was a few weeks before Gene heard from Jenni again. They ran into each other at the grocery store again, but this time not literally.

"Gene! I'm so glad to see you. Um, would you mind helping me with my genealogy again? I've been busy lately but want to get back to that Alford problem."

Gene and Jenni planned to meet at Gene's house this time.

***

Jenni sat staring at what looked like a file cabinet explosion. They were in Gene's home office. Gene decided she'd let Jenni see this disaster so they could try out one of Gene's favorite techniques, using a whiteboard.

Gene started taking papers off her magnetic whiteboard and stuffing them in a folder.

"Oh, Gene, you don't need to clean up. It's fine."

Gene laughed, "I'm not cleaning up. I wanted to use the whiteboard. That's why I invited you into this mess."

As Gene started erasing the lines on the board, Jenni asked, "But won't you lose track of what you were doing?"

"No. I just like to try to look at records in a different way. Putting them on the whiteboard helps me see more than I can see on a computer monitor. I've got notes of anything I'll need later."

"Of course. That might be the most valuable thing I've learned from you!"

"Thanks. I'm so glad to hear I've helped. So what are you stuck on, then? Are you still having problems with your plan?"

"No. Not exactly. You know, I started working on an actual report on my Alford problem."

Gene nodded in the affirmative, so Jenni continued, "It was amazingly helpful. I'm not saying it didn't take a while, but I could tell I wasn't repeating the same thing over and over again but making progress. And by the way, I *had* found the database entry for Henry's death. Way back when I started years ago. I found a file folder I started and never looked at again." Jenni's face clouded over at the thought of the time she wasted repeating the research she had in that folder. "But even going over everything, I can't come up with any other sources to use for this Alford problem. I just feel like there must be some other sources out there. I think I'm going to take an online course or maybe go to a conference or institute so I learn more about doing genealogy in general, but surely I can come up with some source ideas before that happens!"

"I've got another trick to help you with this, Jenni."

"Great, I love your tricks."

Jenni needs to identify other sources. Keep reading to learn the trick Gene teaches her.

***

Jenni has some great ideas for how to find *a father*, but they aren't the best ideas for finding *Henry's father*. She's now reviewed her past research, and she knows as much about what sources she's already used as she can at this point. She needs some different ideas for possible sources, and she simply doesn't know how to come up with them.

Before you learn the trick Gene teaches her, let's consider why Jenni needs to come up with ideas for new sources instead of using the ideas she already had. In previous chapters, we've looked at what researching Henry's religion could look like. That's some very involved research. But what about checking for an Alford marriage for Henry's possible mother? This is likely something Jenni is interested in, even if it doesn't solve her current problem.

Jenni doesn't have a location for the marriage, just a likely area. Research into marriages in an area is unlikely to provide clues aside from determining no marriage was recorded in that location. That's little information for a lot of work. Jenni can search marriages in an area in Alabama but with marriage records, you either find a marriage record, or you don't. Every time you don't find a marriage, you also don't find clues. Other types of research don't work this way. Sometimes it's necessary to do research where you're mainly finding nothing, such as searching for a marriage record.

But that's not Jenni's current question, so first, she can try generating ideas for additional sources.

Gene uses four basic ways to think about new sources, and she's going to teach Jenni, and you, these options.

Tons of sources exist, potentially with the evidence or clues you need. First, you want to focus on sources you can access, and this trick is designed to do that. Ideally, sources are accessed soon, but you may have to identify sources you can access in the near future or with a bit of planning or budgeting. What Jenni had tried was just learning about sources. This didn't take into account what she could access.

Here's how Gene suggests she approach identifying new sources.

#1 Focus on Repositories

The best way to learn about sources you can access *soon* is by focusing on repositories you can access. As discussed when we talked about citing online websites, a repository is any place that holds sources. That can be a library or archive. It can be a website. It can be your house or a relative's house.

A repository holds sources, and sources hold information. A person can be a source; think of them as a repository. An embroidered sampler can be a source. The family Bible is a source. A birth certificate is a source. A written family history is a source. School records can be a source. Court records can be a source. You can find these sources in all kinds of places, and those places are a repository.

Ask yourself what repositories you can access. When Jenni considered ordering the death certificate, the repository was Alabama Vital Records. She would mail a request to them. Even though she wasn't physically visiting, that was the repository, and it was accessible to her by mail. Accessing a source without visiting the repository means using the mail, a third-party website, or an actual third-party—such as hiring a researcher to get a record for you. This strategy about accessible repositories still holds regardless of the access method. Jenni may not be able to visit Alabama soon but she can mail a request for the death certificate so that record is accessible.

If you have an internet connection, FamilySearch.org is the largest free online genealogy website. Most of its sources—the digitized records—are *not* searchable. You browse them, which is the digital equivalent of using microfilm or an unindexed book. Browsing records means they aren't as low-hanging fruit as a record you can search with a form, but they are free and online, making them very accessible.

Definitions

Browse: To browse online images of sources; you go image by image to find the information you need. This is like reading page by page in an unindexed book or browsing microfilm, which is where the term came from. You browse microfilm by cranking the handle to get to the image on the film you want. Browsing online images is much easier on the arm than using a manual microfilm reader.

Database: A searchable online structure that holds information. Fields in a search form should match the fields in a database. If they don't, those database fields are either not being used for a search, or the search form fields are searching multiple database fields. This affects your search results, so it is important to understand. Databases often provide good search results, but they can contain typos.

OCR: Optical character recognition allows you to search records that don't have a database. Sometimes a database is created from an automated OCR search. An example is the collection "U.S. City Directories, 1822-1995" on Ancestry. The computer does an automated OCR search to fill in the database fields which you can then search using a search form. Often the street address appears in the street address field, but sometimes it appears as a name or other field. It can be garbled because the computer read the information, not a human. This applies to all the fields and information in this collection. This information was compiled into the database by an automated OCR search rather than a person reading the information and typing it into the database. The alternative is an unsearchable collection you can only browse, not a human-created database.

With OCR, essentially, the computer tries to read the text and match it to your search. If the text is hard to read or the letters look similar, an OCR search can produce very different results than you want. Remember, this is a computer trying to read. A human might correctly interpret similarly shaped letters because one makes a common name or word and the other doesn't. A computer doesn't make this distinction. Different search techniques should be used for an OCR search versus a database search.

Important! Some *databases* also allow you to browse all the records, but some can only be searched. If a search doesn't give you results you know are in a database, you may be able to browse to find what you want. If an OCR search doesn't provide results you know are in that record, you can try altering your search, or you may need to browse the records. Knowing if you need to browse or can browse is just as important as knowing if you can search and what type of search is being performed.

Millions of online source images can be accessed for free but are not searchable. Probably millions of searchable records exist that don't search perfectly. Now that you've learned about browsable images, searchable databases, and searchable OCR images, you might want to reuse some past sources. Certainly, don't say you're done with a problem or source just from performing a search, though.

In addition to the millions of free browsable images, some images aren't free, both searchable and not. You can find online images with limited search functionality, some are free, and some are not. Online records are easy to access when you compare them to options involving travel or hiring someone to research for you. You can learn about easy-to-access sources by learning about what sources an accessible repository, such as a website, has.

If you are paying for a subscription, like Ancestry, that is a repository you can use. *Always assume there are additional sources that are not searchable on a website.* Repository sites like Ancestry have many records that won't appear in a search. But even if the result you need does come up in a search, the result might be on the 103rd page of search results, so you don't see it. You can find unsearchable results or results that end up way down the results list by looking for a *source*, not searching a *repository*.

Focusing on identifying specific sources within a repository can change your search results. You might find results buried low in search results of the entire repository, or you might discover browse-only sources that contain just what you were looking for.

Don't forget to consider physical repositories you can visit, like your local library, a relative's attic or storage unit, a nearby courthouse or archive, etcetera. At a physical repository, you need to decide what sources *might* contain information that can help you. Remember, you want clues, not just answers. You presumably already looked for an answer and didn't find it; that's why you're stuck.

Try approaching online repositories the same way you'd use a physical library or archive. If you remember learning to do research in a physical library, you didn't have an option to just search for what you needed. You had to identify books and then use each one to see if they would help. Some helped, and some didn't. You didn't know which until you used that source. That's how genealogy works!

Think of websites as you'd think of a 20th-century library. The website is like a whole library, not one book. You don't try to search for everything in one go at the library. In a 20th-century-style library, you identify specific books and use them. Treat online repositories the same way, and you'll find a lot more clues!

FYI: Most genealogy websites have something like a card catalog. Start with the repository strategy and use the card catalog or equivalent finding aid to identify "sources" within the repository.

Takeaway: Recognize the difference between a repository and a source. Using individual sources will produce different results than searching a repository. Different types of online searches as well as non-searchable sources, can be used. Use the best approach based on the specifics of the individual source. A great way to find more sources is by identifying the repositories you can access and then seeing what sources they hold. You likely need to look into individual sources at repositories you've already used if you only searched at the repository level.

#2 Focus on Location

You absolutely must learn about the records created for the location where you are researching. You might be missing *the answer* because you didn't learn about a record commonly created in that location. This is always true, but focusing on a location is one of the most basic tenants of genealogy research. It's not strategy number one because starting with repositories helps you identify easily accessible sources first.

Once you identify your accessible repositories, you often next see what sources they have for your research location. That is strategy one combined with strategy two. Strategy two is slightly different, where you first learn about sources for the location.

You may find additional online, local, or easily accessible sources you missed when you focus on the location rather than the repository. Many local jurisdictions, like a county or state, or even small physical repositories have online records. You might miss these when only focusing on repositories, but you easily discover them once you're looking for a type of record for a specific location. Also, sometimes sources cover multiple locations or are cataloged under a different or wrong location. When you start with a repository and see what they have for your location, you may miss these options. Looking for records you have learned should exist will often reveal relevant sources you missed when using the repository strategy.

Don't skimp on locations.

Every person you research will have multiple relevant locations, even if they only lived in one place and never left. In the U.S., you will have the following:

- The country, federal records
- The state or territory before statehood
- The county or parish in Louisiana

You might also or instead have a city, town, or religious parish. It's vital to learn what types of jurisdictions controlled the events that could happen during a person's life. These can vary dramatically from one location to the other, which is why focusing on locations, and learning about specific ones, is so important in genealogy.

For colonial America and locations outside the U.S., you will have multiple locations as well. It is up to you to learn which ones apply to your research subject. Before online research, this was basic knowledge every genealogist at least got started with. It's just as important in the 21st-century. You could let the computer do the basics when you started, so you may or may not have learned about research locations.

Fast and Easy Option to Start Learning About Research Locations

If you are just getting started using FamilySearch.org, use the catalog to browse records for the locations your person lived in. Also, checkout the Wiki entry for the primary jurisdiction they lived under. The primary jurisdiction is the location that created the most records for them. For 19th-century Americans, this is frequently a county unless they lived where town records were predominant. It could also be a territory or even the U.S. depending on the exact time and place.

Records will be found under the location where they were created. Most records for U.S. research are not found under the U.S.; they are under the county, town, or state. Where my ancestors lived in Georgia, no town records were kept— town records exist in Georgia, just not where my ancestors lived. However, you'll find private records listed under the town on FamilySearch. These are often church records, but they can be all sorts of things. It's easy to browse the *FamilySearch Catalog* to learn about various options. This is a simple, free place to start!

Learn More

You may have already employed this location strategy if you've learned about topics like "German Research," "Irish Immigration," and so forth. That education might have included information on researching based on religion or other commonly shared characteristics, but it probably also included researching a location—Germany or Ireland. Think about what you learned and how you could learn similar information about other locations, such as a country, state, parish, county, or region.

If you already know about researching the largest location, such as a country, try learning about a more specific region. Depending on the timeframe and country, this will vary. Too many genealogists don't get specific enough when researching people outside their primary country. This could be the primary country your research subjects lived in or *your* residence—the country you have personal experience with jurisdictions.

This is particularly an issue for Americans since most Americans have immigrant ancestors they research at some point. Even if you have all American colonial lines, the jurisdictions for colonial America can be very different from what you are familiar with for U.S. research. Make sure you learn about the appropriate locations and jurisdictions for your specific problem.

If you have 18th-century Germans, learning about how 20th-century German records were kept won't help much. For one thing, "Germany" didn't exist! You need to know what kind of locations existed when your ancestor lived in that location. Within those locations, what types of records were normally created? Then you can learn if those records should or do exist for the exact time and place you are researching.

For example, can you get a book of town births for the exact town and time frame when your ancestor should have been born? Sometimes you need to start researching to determine if the exact record exists; sometimes, you can find a list of what records exist. This doesn't tell you if your ancestor is in the record, but if the records don't exist, you know to try something else.

Important! Always learn the details when you see "all the records were destroyed." This roadblock mostly relates to location, but the details make a huge difference. Once upon a time, I read an old genealogy article that said the county clerk kept telling researchers no records survived—they were all burned during the Civil War. This article was published when most people contacted the county clerk to do research in that county versus using microfilm or online records. That county became known as a "burned county." However, only a few records were lost due to this Civil War fire. The fire happened, but most of the records survived. The details made a huge difference.

You need to know the details. Different kinds of disasters or record losses result in different extant records. Many European researchers have to deal with the destruction of towns during WWII. It is possible everything in the town was lost. That means courthouse records, newspaper records, church records, and private records. But often, a whole town isn't destroyed. Only records in one location are lost, such as just the courthouse or just the church. No matter the situation, you need to consider other locations, as we've already discussed.

Here's an example: Early U.S. pension records were lost due to fire. That destroyed federal records. But pensioners may have gotten an affidavit from their local court. That record may still exist in the county court record book. It isn't the whole pension but not everything was lost, just the federal records. The details related to locations help you find potential records *and* potential alternatives when significant record loss happens.

Reminder: Take notes so you don't waste time looking for the same record that doesn't exist later. Also, note if a record isn't currently accessible but might be available later. Some repositories have rules preventing access to records for a variety of reasons. These rules or the circumstances can change, such as a privacy time limit running out after a certain date. If you have good notes, you'll know if you *should* try to get the source again.

#3 Focus on Record Type

As a genealogist, you need to learn about *types of records* and what information they might contain. Record types can be marriage records or broader church records. It could be wills, broader probate records, or even broader court records. By learning about what kind of information different types of records contain, you will have an idea of what potential records could provide clues to your specific problem.

For example: If you want to find a date of birth, birth records aren't the only choice. Vital records (birth, marriage, and death) aren't your only choice. Religious, school, occupational, military, fraternal, and more and more records could all potentially provide the *answer* of a birth date. It's unlikely all of these exist for your person or that all of them provide an answer. They all potentially provide clues, just as census records might provide a clue.

Genealogists need to know which sources are most likely to provide an answer and then which are most likely to provide the best clues. Keep checking anything you think might provide a clue if you haven't solved your problem. Don't stop at "most likely to provide an answer" and give up when that doesn't work. You want to know what is most likely to help, to prioritize what sources to use, not so you have an excuse for stopping. Knowing what types of records are most likely to contain an answer starts with low-hanging fruit, and it's the sensible thing to do. It's not the only thing to do.

Thinking by record type is similar to thinking by location. With location, your ancestor lived in a country, but they probably had a local jurisdiction that created records about them, too. You have to identify the various larger and smaller locations that are relevant, and it's similar with types of records.

Birth and death records are grouped together as vital records. Vital records aren't the same as religious records, which can include baptism and burial records. A baptism record can be an alternative to a birth record, and a burial record might be an alternative to a death record. Burial records might be religious, or they might be private or civil—when the burial was overseen by the town or other civil location or by the private cemetery or funeral home.

Thinking about sources by record type is a type of analysis. When you're stuck, you presumably start thinking by asking questions. "I need to find his birth date. Where can I find that?" You'd probably think, "Where's his birth certificate?" When you think by record type, you can think about birth records, baptisms, and so on, or you can think, "What vital records exist for this time and place?" or "Are there religious records" or "Did I check court records?"

Once you learn about what types of genealogy records exist, this becomes much easier. Trying to think by record type can also be a way to gain that knowledge. The list of ideas Jenni had for her first research plan was thinking by record type. She made a list of ideas to find Henry's father. She was thinking about records that could have information about who someone's father was.

Focusing on record type is probably the more reusable type of source information for many genealogists. For this reason, store this information in notes and remember what you can, so you don't have to read a book or scour the internet to gather the same details whenever you need them. Gene encouraged Jenni to make a note about how the tax records might help identify Henry's father. If she can remember that detail, she can use it quicker for a future project than if she needs to find the file containing her note. Putting it in her notes will help her remember it as well as being a back-up if she forgets the specifics. It is probably faster for her to find her note than trying to find that information by scouring the internet, too.

Store information about sources in notes for future reference. Record type is the most generic and, therefore, reusable of the options in this chapter, so it is what you are most likely to look up again. Saving it, even if you don't save information about locations or repositories, should save you the most time. You'll probably remember some of what you learned, but it may be the details you forgot that you need most. Notes are the place for these details.

Hint: I save this type of information to Evernote. For me, I know that's where I store this kind of genealogy information, and it takes less than a minute to save it and add tags so I can find it again. This allows me to skip taking notes about a source—not information from a source, just information about sources. I save the webpage or snap a picture of the information and store it in Evernote. If only all research was this simple!

While researching, if you come across a type of record that you don't know what it is or where or when it would have been created, try to learn. Sources often have some type of explanatory information attached if they are online or abstracted or transcribed into a published book. Once again, FamilySearch.org contains a ton of free information to help you learn the basics.

Important! When dealing with large amounts of record loss for a location, you combine alternative jurisdictions with alternative types of records. This has already been touched on. Record loss might be for all records in a location, but it is more common for it to apply to a repository. If the courthouse burned, that doesn't mean the newspaper office burned. Even if the whole town burned, maybe older church records had been sent to a different repository, so they were not in the town at that time. It is your responsibility as a great genealogist to learn this information *as you need it.*

Focusing on records by record type can be a big undertaking. Starting with one repository or a specific location is more focused. Eventually, you want to learn about types of genealogy records because that does help you think of the most potential sources. It's just not the easiest or most efficient place to start when you want to solve a particular problem.

#4 Focus on Time Period

Contemplating time periods is probably the least effective way to think about sources when you get stuck. Sometimes time periods work well, but not always. Once you've tried the other approaches, you should try this one.

Usually, if you learn about records by time period, you'll need to add a location. You can learn about 20th-century U.S. records or colonial American records, or various time periods in other countries. Some time-place combos are hard to learn about.

You probably won't find a quick educational source to learn about 19th-century U.S. sources because of the number of records and their variations. By the 20th-century most states existed, whereas in the 19th-century, the country was expanding, and many territories came and went. In colonial America, fewer locations existed, so it's possible to summarize your options, although it's faster to focus on New England or individual states.

For other countries, focusing on a time period for that country might work well. You need some idea of the history of an area to decide if you can learn about sources by time period.

Best Source Research Strategy: Mix It Up

Finally, the best way to come up with potential new sources is to combine these options. The most accessible sources you find at your accessible repositories. Start with accessibility and then add either location or record type to identify specific sources. From the location or record type, you can narrow your options by time period or record type and location—whichever you haven't already used.

You can also start by learning about types of sources for the location-time combo. It might be pretty easy to learn about types of sources once you narrow it to a time and place, but you might need to focus on records for something unique about your ancestor. For example, you might be to the point that you need to see what Baptist records exist for postbellum Mississippi. Maybe you need to learn about Jewish records in early 20th-century New York City. Those are specific types of records in a specific time and place. Often you don't stumble across these records until you're looking for either the type or location.

Genealogists need to spend time researching the *existence* of records, not just researching *in* the records. Also, never forget that most records aren't online. The most widely used records—widely used before they were online—are what get digitized. Your ancestor is one person, though. What makes him or her unique might be a combination of unusual characteristics. They might appear in a lot of records, but those records might be in small collections, private collections, or just collections that the owner doesn't want digitized.

Once you have an idea of what kinds of records to look for, you are far more likely to be able to get the records that do exist, even if they aren't online. With online records, once you go looking for specific records, you're more likely to find your ancestor than only by searching a repository.

Chapter 14:
Is it a Problem?

"OK, Gene, what you're telling me is I can try these four ways to come up with ideas for sources. Right? I use places I have access to. I focus on location and learn about what records exist for Alabama or even the specific counties. I learn about record types that can help me identify a father, which I already tried, or I focus my research in the late 19th-century?"

"That's right. Just remember, sometimes you should instead work on a sub-problem or related research. For your Alford problem, you should probably just learn about what sources you can access with your paid subscription, free online records, and what you can use at the local libraries in the area.

"I'll tell you, our county does have a genealogy room, but you should try one of the counties closer to the city. Several have a lot of resources available. We've also got a few historical societies, history centers, and the state archive. I know your problem is for Alabama, but all of these provide free access to some paid subscription sites when you're in the building. If you can't make that trip to Alabama soon, you've got plenty of local options."

"That sounds a bit overwhelming."

"It could be. I found it fun to learn what was available at each of them and try to figure out if they had anything unique. There was one local library that had this huge collection of Virginia genealogy books. But, they didn't have much other material compared to most of the public libraries in our area. I asked a librarian, and she said someone willed those books from their personal collection. You never know what you'll find until you look."

"Hmm. I have some Virginia research I haven't worked on. It might be fun to go there for a day trip. I could use a break from this Alford problem."

"That's not a bad idea. Working on another problem can give you new ideas."

"I don't know that I have the energy to try to organize that Virginia research like I've done with the Alford problem. I'd want a break from it before I got to the library if I wrote so many reports again!"

"I understand. There is another approach to research we haven't talked about. It's not about solving a problem. It's still something you need to do sometimes. In fact, if you happened to be at a library with unique resources, it's likely what you'd do. What are the odds you'd unintentionally find yourself somewhere that had the records you needed for a problem you had W-frame defined, reviewed, and completely updated? You'd be at that library on purpose, not by chance. I don't like to waste a research opportunity, so I use this other approach to take advantage of sources I'm not ready to use with a full research plan."

"That sounds interesting. I don't quite understand, but it sounds interesting."

Learn the distinction between solving a problem and doing genealogy tasks in the following section. Understanding the difference can make you a more successful genealogist.

***

Earlier in the book, I mentioned the research process is for solving problems, not other types of genealogy tasks. This is not a complicated distinction, but it is important to recognize. If you try to apply the W-frame system and research planning to *tasks,* you may struggle. But it's often just a waste of time. Trying to do too much can make you abandon the research process, and I don't want that for you.

So, you always need to write *it* down in genealogy, no matter what *it* is. If you don't take notes, it's like it didn't happen. I don't mean the ancestor's birth; I mean the time you spent working on whatever you worked on. Do you have time you are willing to throw away that way? But writing it down isn't always creating a research plan or having a W-frame-defined problem.

Now that I've emphasized making notes of whatever you do, what's the problem? Or is it not a problem but a genealogy task?

Tasks Aren't a Problem

I use the term "genealogy tasks" to mean genealogy work you do that isn't necessarily research or related to solving a specific problem. This was less common before online research because it was so much harder to do. Sometimes it is research, but it requires less thought, so I like to make it a distinct action.

Rather than describe the task, here are examples:

- Finding all the census records an ancestor appeared in.
- Finding a source for all the marriages for a group of people, such as a set of siblings.
- Citing sources for the research on a specific ancestor.
- Creating quick and dirty trees for DNA matches.
- Finding burial places for as many ancestors as possible.
- Checking for additional voyages for an immigrant ancestor.
- Looking for ancestors in a certain type of record, for example, checking the printed Revolutionary War Pension Index for all appropriate ancestors instead of the online pensions because you have so many surnames like Williams that also produce results as a first name.

Some of the examples above are research, such as finding marriages, but some aren't, such as citing sources. The commonality in all of these items is that they're tasks you are trying to complete, not problems you are trying to solve.

We all have different amounts and types of time available to us. I can tell you my genealogy skills have vastly improved over the years by spending some of my smaller amounts of time doing tasks instead of working on a problem. Sometimes knocking out a task can provide unexpected information that helps with a problem. Sometimes it just helps make your brain *whir* a little differently, and you suddenly make progress on a problem that had you stumped.

Focusing on a task like citing sources improves your citation skills differently than citing your sources while following the research process. This is another example of context switching. If you want to improve your citation skills, that skill will improve faster by focusing on it instead of sandwiching it between research and review work. If you want to solve a problem, you will solve it faster by focusing on the problem, not focusing on only finding burial records, then census records, then marriage records. In genealogy, you could say you are always context switching. With so many pieces to genealogy, your brain is always switching between something. The point is to minimize context switching for your intention. Do you intend to solve a problem or complete a simpler task?

The point is tasks are not a genealogy problem. Another important piece of this distinction is that often the research process doesn't work for tasks. You still need to make notes of what you are doing, but you may or may not be focused on a W-frame-defined problem. A specific problem could provide the group of people you focus your task on. Creating an actual research plan for tasks is rarely necessary. You may want to make a list or description of what you are trying to do so you can track your progress. This provides the function of a plan but doesn't need the same template parts of a plan.

One thing I have heard from multiple struggling genealogists is how difficult the research process is. This perspective generally comes from ones that seem to struggle perpetually by applying the research process to tasks. This can happen because they are so inexperienced they struggle to recognize the problem they are trying to solve. They can understand how to gather a type of information from a source they are familiar with, so that is the work they decide to do. But if they try to apply the entire research process to this task, it is a lot of extra work.

You don't need a full research plan to search online for census records for one person. You can create a plan, but what's your hypothesis? The person appears in census records? Your why is finding them in each census they appear in. That seems repetitive. Practicing creating a research plan for a task can hamper your learning because it doesn't work quite right. I can't even develop a reasonable hypothesis for a narrow and actionable plan where the idea is to find every census record for one person. That action is doing a task, not solving a problem. But if you haven't recognized this distinction, you might think you are bad at creating hypotheses or that it is just too hard to mess with.

Applying the research process to a task makes the task seem harder than it needs to be. You might do it successfully. That's not the point. Don't abandon the research process based on your experience with genealogy tasks. Treat completing tasks differently than problem-solving. You still need notes, and you need to track research if your task is research. Make sure you can find the results of your task for any problem it will be related to. That is how you know you're doing enough note-taking, tracking, and organizing for a task. Your task notes should be reviewed for appropriate problems even though they are created outside of working on a problem.

Also, ensure you aren't trying to solve a genealogy problem solely by doing tasks. Tasks gather information, often the same types of information for multiple people. Hard problems require you to approach research from a different direction. With a task, you know what you are looking for. With a problem, you often need to find what you didn't know you needed. The research process is designed to aid you in doing this, although it takes practice. Most importantly, doing tasks doesn't provide the review of a specific problem that is needed to bust a brick wall. Tasks might gather all the information, but you will likely overlook a solution since tasks don't put the information together with other information. That's what the research process excels at.

Tasks are an essential part of genealogy, but they are only a part. Problem-solving is also only a part of genealogy. Use both. Organize your results so you can use them whenever needed. Research tasks generate information needed for problem-solving. Problem-solving, going through the research process, will generate tasks that must be done. These might be research tasks, but they can also be education or organization tasks. Tasks aren't a problem so don't treat them like one.

Conclusion

Doing *great* genealogy doesn't happen overnight. You've seen how Jenni started out with a bunch of genealogy search results she attached to a tree and nothing else. Through this book, you've learned the skills you can build on top of each other to go from being a no-notes Jenni to a research process Jenni—from a beginner to a great genealogist.

Because you can't just suddenly do all these things, many must be learned and practiced; they weren't presented in the order you'll do them once you are skilled at everything. They were presented in the order you needed to learn them, so you were committed to doing each additional type of work.

Now it's time to look at the whole process and also set realistic expectations depending on where you are with your skills. A few more topics need to be fleshed out now that we see the whole research process, but much of this information is a recap.

First, we have a choose-your-own-adventure recap that depends on your personal situation.

All genealogists need to review the research related to the problem they want to solve. Your personal situation majorly affects how you can realistically start doing this *today*. Ideally, you'll eventually review the reports to yourself and refer back to your notes or document copies only when needed. But you have to have reports, and reports covering everything, before you can review them. So today, you need to choose what you can do to start working towards the faster, more successful, *great* genealogy state you'll eventually be in.

The Getting Started Option

If you've never taken notes or feel your overall genealogy process is erratic, even if you've tried note-taking, reporting, or planning, start by committing to take genealogy notes. If you take paper notes, you will also need to keep a research log. If you take digital notes, be sure to include all the information we discussed that should be tracked. Get good at taking notes by reviewing the sources you've already used and taking notes for your past research. This will recreate the tracking information as much as possible after the fact. Remember to meet the W-frame requirements for each problem you are focusing on.

A Money Saving Option

Consider pausing paid subscriptions while you focus on reviewing past research. Download copies of relevant records, stop or pause your subscription(s), and review the copies, taking notes, of course. Or you can plan to pause paid subscriptions in the future so you can focus on free records you never looked into. Don't overlook paid subscriptions you can access at your local library or other local repositories, too.

When you pay for a subscription, you want to get your money's worth. This often encourages fast and sloppy research. If you can arrange to save money on subscriptions while improving your review process, this is a win-win. It's not always possible since you may need your paid subscription to perform a good review, but it's something to consider!

Keep Going

Once you're tracking research and consistently taking notes, whether you have just started or have already been doing this, make sure you start planning your research. Use the Genealogy Roll-up if you take digital notes to save the maximum amount of time and create the best results for your future reviews.

Also, once you're tracking your research and consistently taking notes, remember to work analysis into your process. Decide what is appropriate for you. Very basic analysis to meet the W-frame requirements may be where you are. You might be a naturally analytical person. If you are, focus on reviewing and learning more ways to do genealogical analysis. Learning plus doing *new* research is a lot at once. Reviewing gives you practical experience using what you're learning while helping you move at a pace where your process isn't cheated from new-research excitement.

The Research Alternatives in the Roadmap

Finally, once you're comfortable with whatever you are adding to your genealogy research process, whether that's tracking research, note-taking, planning, reporting, or even reviewing, make sure you're also staying motivated to do great genealogy—bring in education and organization.

Education

Some genealogists need to emphasize learning. Organize that learning with an education plan. This can be as simple as creating a "to-read" list. Include lectures, webinars, classes, and courses in your education plan. You can also create something more involved by creating an education budget. If you spend money on genealogy education, especially the amount of money needed for institutes, conferences, or longer online courses, create a budget for that education, even if your education plan is a simple list. Create an education plan using a format and method easy for you to create, update, and use.

Organization

Some genealogists need to emphasize slowing down. If it's a constant battle for you to spend your genealogy time on anything other than searching online, organization can help. This doesn't mean you need to recreate your genealogy filing system, although if you don't have a system for organizing your genealogy, you do need one. Organize your genealogy time, similar to organizing work time.

If you successfully organize your time and tasks for your job, volunteer work, housework, or any use of your time where you accomplish tasks that need to be done, regardless of whether you want to do them, use the same method for your genealogy time.

If you aren't successfully organizing your time, start keeping a genealogy to-do list. Spend a small portion of your genealogy time keeping this list current. Also, spend a portion of your genealogy time on education, a small portion on organizing your results, a lot of your genealogy time on reviewing, a small portion on research planning, and finally, a small portion on research. Yes, only a small portion of your total time on actual research.

You don't need to do all these items every week if you spend some time weekly, or monthly if you have limited time. Though it sounds ironic, the less time you have, the less time you should spend researching. Instead, become a *research planning* ninja and take advantage of every shortcut you can. You learn planning strategies through education, hence spending time learning even if you don't have much time.

Also, when you have limited time, your results must be better organized. At first, that may mean learning to organize your results better. Eventually, create a system to ensure everything stays organized so you can review as fast as is reasonable when you return to a problem. This page on *The Occasional Genealogist* blog contains links to posts related to organizing your genealogy time, including keeping a genealogy to-do list, https://bit.ly/genealogy-to-do-list.

You can do great genealogy. It requires a great process, which has long existed, and you now know and understand.

It also requires practice. This is great news for genealogists because "practice" means you need to do genealogy. You love doing genealogy!

Finally, remember genealogy is *building* a family tree. You keep adding to what you previously did. Every genealogist also starts as a new genealogist. No matter your education or work experience, you didn't start your family tree as an experienced family historian. If you haven't reviewed and updated your past work, you may be building on a shaky foundation. Your family tree is full of different problems, and you can get all of them to a place where you're doing great genealogy. The genealogy research process is designed for this situation because it's something every genealogist shares. Combining a great process, education, organization, and genealogy tasks is something *you* can do for great genealogy.

ABOUT THE AUTHOR

 Jennifer Patterson Dondero has been an avid genealogist for over 30 years, and a professional genealogist since 2005. Her specialties include southern research, DNA, technology for genealogy, and of course, research shortcuts for Occasional Genealogists. She lives with her husband and two children in Georgia, where she enjoys reading and writing mystery novels, Irish dancing, and clogging. You can learn more from her on how to do your own family research at www. TheOccasionalGenealogist.com.

Can You Help?

Thank You For Reading My Book!

I hope it helped you grow your family tree.

Help other genealogists know if this is the right book for them.

Please leave me an honest review on Amazon.

I really appreciate all of your feedback, and I love hearing what you have to say.

Thanks so much!

Jennifer

Self-Publishing School

NOW IT'S YOUR TURN

Discover the EXACT 3-step blueprint you need to become a bestselling author in as little as 3 months.

Self-Publishing School helped me, and now I want them to help you with this FREE resource to begin outlining your book**!**

Even if you're busy, bad at writing, or don't know where to start, you CAN write a bestseller and build your best life.

With tools and experience across a variety of niches and professions,

Self-Publishing School is the <u>only</u> resource you need to

take your book to the finish line!

DON'T WAIT

Say "YES" to becoming a bestseller:

https://self-publishingschool.com/friend/

Follow the steps on the page to get a FREE resource to get started on your book and unlock a discount to get started with Self-Publishing School

Made in the USA
Middletown, DE
06 September 2024

60419660R00157